CW00739083

DEATH IN

A Typical Fighting Squadron in France

(Photograph copyright by Imperial War Museum)

DEATH IN THE AIR

THE WAR DIARY AND PHOTOGRAPHS
OF A FLYING CORPS PILOT

WESLEY D. ARCHER

FRONTLINE BOOKS

Death in the Air

A Greenhill Book

Published in 1985 by Greenhill Books, Lionel Leventhal Limited
www.greenhillbooks.com

This edition published in 2016 by

Frontline Books
an imprint of Pen & Sword Books Ltd,
47 Church Street, Barnsley, S. Yorkshire, S70 2AS
For more information on our books, please visit
www.frontline-books.com, email info@frontline-books.com
or write to us at the above address.

ISBN: 978-1-84832-878-5

Publishing History
Death in the Air: The War Diary and Photographs of a Flying Corps Pilot was first published in 1933.

CIP data records for this title are available from the British Library

Printed and bound by CPI Group (UK) Ltd, Croydon, CR0 4YY

INTRODUCTION

Death in the Air was first published, to acclaim, in 1933 and became a best seller. The photographs, especially, attracted attention for no one had ever seen such pictures of dog-fighting, with the planes so close, and the sense of action so breathtaking.

There was mystery surrounding *Death in the Air* for over fifty years. The source of the photographs has however now been established by Peter Grosz and Karl Schneide, working at the National Air and Space Museum in Washington, DC. Edwards Park, Contributing Editor of *Smithsonian Magazine*, has written in detail the story of the exposure of the origin of *Death in the Air*. This Introduction is based upon the *Smithsonian Magazine* article.

The origin of *Death in the Air* lies with a 1931 exhibition of aviation art, which included "The Cockburn-Lange Collection". This attracted enormous attention, including a double-page spread in *The Illustrated London News* under the headline: "The Most Extraordinary Photographs Ever Taken of Air Fights in the War". *Death in the Air* was published soon afterwards.

Early on, doubt was cast about the authenticity of the photographs, but "Mrs. Cockburn-Lange" avoided meetings to discuss them and in post-World

War I Britain the privacy of a widow of a war hero was respected.

The source of the content for the book remained a mystery for fifty years until 1983. In that year the Smithsonian's National Air and Space Museum took delivery of several large suitcases, a donation from eighty-six year old John W. Charlton of Gloversville, New York. "The bags contained stacks of letters", wrote Edwards Park in his article in *Smithsonian Magazine*, "and news clippings, a .45 Colt automatic with a dent in it, World War I aviator uniforms, a 1918 camera and various other items. They had belonged to Charlton's lifelong friend, a World War I fighter pilot named Wesley David Archer. No one at the Air and Space Museum had ever heard of him."

Peter Grosz happened upon the acquisition, almost by accident, and recognised some of the photographs as originals from the "Cockburn-Lange Collection". Grosz enlisted the help of Karl Schneide and the two men began sorting out the letters and clippings – and 109 Cockburn-Lange negatives. They established that "Cockburn-Lange" was a pseudonym for the wife of Archer and turned their attention to him. Wesley Archer had indeed been a World War I pilot; an American serving with the RAF (his parents were Canadian), he joined what was still known as the Royal Flying Corps in 1917. On 9th October 1918 he was shot down by ground fire while strafing German infantry in his SE5. A bullet headed for his heart was deflected by his Colt automatic – the badly dented one now at the Museum. Photographs of Archer show a rather dashing young man.

Archer convalesced in Britain, returned to the United States in 1920 and set about finding something to do. Being clever, restless and creative, he eventually joined the youthful film industry as a set designer and model maker. He even went to Berlin to do miniature sets for movie productions.

In 1927 Wesley and Betty Archer moved up from Florida where they had lived for several years, to New York. Archer and a friend began building the model planes that would feature in his grand illusion – the dramatic hoax that, it is now clear, he was by then planning with meticulous care. He boldly invented personalities for himself and his wife, contrived to safeguard the privacy of "Gladys Maud Cockburn-Lang", legally covered his tracks, and wrote this book.

Grosz and Schneide discovered snapshots of Archer and his friend working with their airplane models. "Interestingly, Archer's honest photographs of the war, taken while he flew with the RFC's 40th Squadron, are excellent. He was a facile writer," writes Edwards Park, himself a former US Army Air Force pilot in World War II. Park says, "Archer's letters are voluminous, descriptive and entertaining. It must have been great fun sitting there in Nyack, writing *Death in the Air* with its telegraphic style, its understated heroics, its flyers' slang. Reading it, you get to know the squadron: Jock, Canada,

Mick, Chilly, Tod, Red, Kaffir and all the others. When one is missing after a run-in with the enemy, you suffer. When the author gets depressed and hits the bottle, you worry. When he meets a girl, you cheer."

The Archers' daring hoax paid off well. Archer claimed he earned 20,000 Depression dollars from the book. "And, perhaps inevitably," wrote Edwards Park, "most of what happened afterwards was an anticlimax. His story, indeed, evokes a sadness that such great skill and talent achieved so little." During World War II he tried to get into the US Army Air Force, but was turned down because of a hernia. Soon after that, the Archers were down and all but out. He was jobless and ill and in a desperate attempt to improve his health and their fortunes, the couple moved to Havana in 1952. Wesley suffered a slight stroke and became entirely dependent upon Betty. Finally, in 1955, he died. The Havana post of the American Legion buried him with full military honours.

Betty Archer – Gladys Maud Cockburn-Lange forsook Cuba and moved to Puerto Rico. Steadfastly, she kept the family secret of the fabricated airman and his startling photographs. When she died in 1959, it was still safe with her.

The Archer memorabilia had been sent by him in the 1950s to a friend who was quite unaware that the photographs had any special significance, and that mystery haunted them. This gentleman however agreed, when interest was shown in the photographs by a neighbour, to entrust them to the National Air and Space Museum. And in doing so led to the solving of a mystery surrounding one of the most famous works of aviation literature.

KARL S. SCHNEIDE
NATIONAL AIR AND SPACE MUSEUM
SMITHSONIAN INSTITUTION

DEATH IN THE AIR

FOREWORD

THE following is printed from a typewritten manuscript of the diary of a pilot, who took most of the accompanying aerial combat photographs, during the War.

Naturally, any entries which would reveal the identity of the squadrons are not contained in this typewritten copy of his journal. It is with regret that these have been deleted, but that was the only condition on which permission could be obtained for its publication.

No attempt has been made to change or improve the phraseology or grammar in the typewritten manuscript, and if at times this is careless is must be borne in mind that the original diary was never written for publication. If, also, his meaning is not always quite clear or comprehensive, the same facts must be remembered. This manuscript is presented in the form which follows exactly that of the original diary, with the exception of certain deletions; and certain vague references, or lack of reference to previous episodes, are not clear even to those who knew this officer.

In many instances in the manuscript there is a lapse of several days, or even weeks, between one entry and the next, i.e., if a Tuesday follows a Monday it must not be taken for granted that it is the following day. Many of the entries in the original diary are not even dated—they merely open with the day of the week.

The pilot was not the swashbuckling, pink-breeched popular conception of the war-time aviator, but one of thousands on both sides of the front line trenches who took their job seriously, not "reasoning why" but "carrying on"; who flew and fought day in and day out, giving and taking, unable in their hearts to harbour that frantic and terrific hatred of the enemy as expressed and shown by some of those who never came in contact with that enemy. Like many other men who "made good" during that time, he was temperate in his drinking, reasonable in his judgment, fulfilling the "daily round and common task" of carrying on as expressed so poignantly in his diary, and in the end dying as he would have wished to die—the death which so many of his friends had died.

His apparently irreligious thoughts may shock the susceptible. It must be borne in mind that he, with millions of others at that time, was daily face-to-face with Death and the grim realities of Life. Under such conditions the religion preached from the safe sanctuary of pew and pulpit, the gospel of brotherly love to all mankind, was but a mockery to those men who faced enemy fire day after day, and held out nothing but false hopes to those to whom the grim, unvarnished realities were what mattered.

At least twelve of the photographs were taken by a brother officer in ——, and no reference can be found in the diary to seven other photographs.

DEDICATED

IN TRIBUTE to those men, both friend and foe, who swept the skies on the wings of death, through storm of wind and rain, snow and hail, ever open to attack, constantly flayed by enemy fire from below and the prey of enemy eagles in the sky.

No radio beacon guided them home when lost. No friendly parachute brought them safely to earth when wounded or aflame. No snug cockpit sheltered them from the merciless elements. Numb with cold, nerves tense to the point of breaking yet ever alert, mindful only of their orders, protecting at all costs their brother pilots, they patrolled the skies day and night, searching through space for the enemy and fighting, far above the clouds, a worthy foe.

To all those pilots who gave their lives for an ideal, and to all those who survived the years of conflict and struggle over the enemy lines, we offer this tribute—the work of those pilots who, through their ingenuity, left behind in photographs a tangible REMEMBRANCE.

ILLUSTRATIONS

THE DIARY

SATURDAY. Nothing but rain and wind, wind and rain, but we fly and curse the elements. When I think of the P.B.I. and what they have to endure this weather am damned thankful I am in R.F.C.; can at least sleep in decent cot and clean bedding. . . . . . .

SUNDAY. Had a taste of real fighting to-day, glad to get back with our skins whole. Ran into big patrol which, instead of running away, split-arsed around and showed some spirit. Fought around the sky for a few minutes and then odds evened up by a flight of Spads from —th Squadron joining in the fracas. Huns soon noticed additional planes and skipped back to their lair. One is down from —th Squadron. Saw him land and climb out of his bus. We were lucky.

MONDAY. Devilish day for flying. . . . . . . Spotted Huns and they saw us at same time. Halberstadts. In a second were circling in pairs. My dancing partner was good pilot and careful. Don't blame him. Chilly kindly picked one of the wasps off my neck, and after a few minutes Huns buzzed off. We didn't follow. All here. Nearly everyone tight, bit wonky myself.

1

TUESDAY. Couple of brief contacts to-day, nothing much. Quirks are hard at it getting photographs and we keep a fatherly eye on them whenever possible. Thank God I'm not a pilot in one of those kites. Old Bard particularly happy to-night, warbling his Scotch ballads.

THURSDAY. Made up for yesterday to-day. Sky at times full of planes and A.A. bursts. Our A.A. put up a couple of puffs near us once and we looked around but couldn't see Huns. Didn't have to wait long, though, to see the reason for the warning bursts. In fraction of second were having lovely set-to and almost at the first brush I got a chance to pot one. Couldn't watch it as I was kept busy preserving my scalp from another one. Scrapped for several minutes and then Pups joined us. Huns soon skipped. At tea-time saw large Hun patrol but kept out of their way. We were a bit nervous as a B.E. below us was doing its bit and if the Huns had seen it they would have made for it. Rumour of some hot work soon, many B.Es. up doing photographic work. They must have nerves of iron to stand such work. Hear Huns overhead.

FRIDAY. Val gone west. Whole squadron silent to-night. Not sure yet whether he is killed or not, but from what we saw there is little chance of his being alive to-night. One of the best, and a crack pilot. Bloody hell and no mistake. We were sent over to bring down a sausage which must have been a favourite of the Huns as they seemed to have it guarded by the entire machine gun corps of their army. Every one of us is riddled like a sieve, and while we got the bloody thing we lost Val. When The Skipper was told on our return he didn't say a word but turned into his hut and only appeared at dinner. He and Val joined up together at the outbreak of war and were old school chums. His old orderly cried like a child in spite of his gray hairs. I didn't see him go down but saw the wreck. Watched for a few seconds as I dodged the bullets but didn't see him crawl out. He was surrounded by infantry in a minute, but we couldn't wait. Everyone getting silently blotto in mess to-night in endeavour to forget that bloody empty chair. Devilish. Blue as Hades. God help the Hun patrol which meets up with us to-morrow morning.

SATURDAY. Didn't have chance to vent spleen until late this afternoon when ran into flock of Huns and gave them what for. Thick heavy clouds gave us a chance to hide and we waited and watched them until favourable chance and then shot into them like dervishes. Vowed I would get one and managed to get on outside of fracas. One of the thick-skulled merchants thought he was in for a meal on this little Britisher but the goose had wings which flew, so he got a surprise. Flew as if I were poor dud and he got careless. Saw chance to pot him and was excitedly pressing triggers when heard cheery old crackle behind me—that Boche was almost sitting on my neck. Threw bus in all directions to get away from him. How little things sober one up at times. Luckily that burst didn't get me. Pure luck. Saw one of the Huns go down in terrific dive. Pilot must have been hit and fallen forward on his stick as his wings left him soon afterwards. Peter got it, lucky beggar. Two Huns were giving Chilly their entire attention, had sense enough to get above one of them and give him a burst. Took his mind off Chilly long enough for him to send other Hun down in flames. Got our revenge alright and I had conceit taken out of me.

TUESDAY. Ground strafed to-day as best we could but difficult work. Fighting is terrific. Not much use at present but we manage to fly somehow. Didn't get a scratch and Huns didn't pester us. They not so keen about flying low as we are. . . . . . .

WEDNESDAY. Peter missing. No planes near us at the time so he must have got archied or a shot from the ground. Were high for machine guns at that time. Anyhow, who knows what happens to a lot of us in this war, and who cares? If they keep on shall soon have no one in the flight. Wish to God weather would become more stable so that we would not be compelled to fly the machine all the time. Too dangerous when you are flying low and have at times to distinguish our own troops. Nearly dropped down on a lot of our men this morning. All I could see were Huns, then saw they were prisoners with our troops. Something told me to look closer before shooting, thank God. Have not given up hope for Peter yet as the wind was blowing almost a gale and he may be down on our side. Hope he is near some troops, bloody cold out in the snow to-night. . . . . . .

FRIDAY. Flew low most of the time in spite of snow storms and wind. Dick, B. Flight, missing. Don't know him very well. Draughts in this bally hut terrific.

SATURDAY. Fought more or less all day. Surprised no one missing. Several scraps, brought down one Hun but doubt if we can chalk it up as we don't know if it was actually destroyed. Holly shot down but got back into our lines unharmed—just arrived back here and feeling himself all over for missing parts.

SUNDAY. Snowing, cold, hellishly uncomfortable

5

flying, but we kept at it. Hun up against it and trying to keep in touch with their fast-retreating infantry, strafing our men also. Faithful old B.E. and R.E.8 boys keep plugging along in their antiquated old traps and we help them whenever we are able to. One brush this afternoon, we were chased home, at least as far as our lines, then Huns got cautious and left us. . . . . . . Have given up hope for old Peter. . . . . . .

SATURDAY. Sky full of Huns, a goodly assortment. Envy the Navy their Tripes. They can turn around inside a champagne bottle. Mixed up with Albatros scouts but they left when Tripes came into it. Albatros are good, sneaking suspicion they are a little better than our Nieups. And they have two guns which is an advantage. Had a jamb once, had a time getting it cleared. The Bard is trying to get Canada to play some rag.

SUNDAY. . . . . . . Time out here is not measured in hours or days, can live a lifetime in few seconds. Did that very thing to-day. In scrap this afternoon suddenly saw tracers tearing past me from everywhere. Two Huns dashed past me—I got lovely bursts from both. Had thought I was pretty good! An experienced pilot! Worthy member of the squadron and a credit to the

R.F.C.! Instead of which discovered almost too late that am good and easy target. Saw holes all over plane and one of the landing wires broken, and, with memory of other day fresh in my mind, was afraid had been hit in vulnerable spot. Queer thoughts raced through my brain and knew I must get back to drome quickly. Feinted a fall out of control, and as I noticed a Hun following me down, hung my arm over side and head down. All the time I was examining the bus for holes. He tried to put more bullets through me but I carefully fell away when thought he was going to shoot. Fortunately engine undamaged, and when I came to few hundred feet from ground Hun didn't follow, stayed higher up and watched for my crash. I suddenly levelled off and scooted towards our lines. Hun, of course, saw move, dived down and spattered lead all around me, but good old bus held together and I zigzagged over the lines and shook him off. Even now can't imagine how I managed to scramble out of that predic. Gods certainly with me that time. No amount of drinks ever gave me such a feeling of nausea in pit of stomach. After I felt safe examined "RIP" more leisurely—found left wing pretty badly sieved. Throttled down and tootled home, trusting to the gods. As I was touching ground in landing felt awful sensation of utter helplessness as she crumpled up and nosed over. All happened so suddenly, got awful bang on nose, knocked me out for few seconds. Someone pouring cognac down my throat choked me into consciousness, grinning mugs of whole squadron woke me up. Afraid old "RIP" will never ride the clouds again.

Monday. Got new plane to-day. Smart work. Hope it will be as faithful a pal as my old "RIP." Transferred some gadgets to new bus so it is not entirely strange. Stripped bullet-riddled cockade from fuselage of first little war horse and now hangs on wall beside me. Queer how attached one becomes to one's bus, like a dog. Faithful old things, they are, stand by one in all sorts of messes. But they got her in the end, as they will get us sooner or later. B. Flight chalked up another Hun to-day.

Tuesday. Whole Hun Flying Corps must be down on this sector. Bloody pugnacious crowd too. Fight like the devil. Lost Con and Derry to-day. Things not so rosy to-night. . . . . . .

Thursday. Another lovely day for squadron. If this keeps up might as well call it off *toute suite*. Understand Pup and Tripe squadrons are not being killed off anything like the way we are. What with ground strafing and Huns flying like devils overhead life is not worth twopence. Another gone to-day, Tyke. Infantry got him.

8

FRIDAY. Sky full of clouds to-day. Poked our noses through before we reached the lines and came out into sunshine like newly-hatched chicks. Archie didn't bother us much, relief. Soon spotted beer stein pals also enjoying beautiful freedom of the skies. Both decided to break monotony about same time. They were about two more than we. Singled out, or rather, was singled out by a dirty looking grey fellow who evidently thought I was a dud. Inadvertently confirmed this opinion by first letting him get a short burst into me, but was not hit in vital spot so kept on and tried to appear nonchalant. He was no novice, as I soon found out. His bursts were short and to the point, if not absolutely conclusive. Second time he tapped me he waved so I waved back. After this exchange of amenities he pulled a funny trick and I lost him for a second, only to see holes being plugged through my wing in a small burst. That boy could shoot straight. Frantically kicked out of it and ended by stalling directly under him. Pressed the trigger and gave him short effective burst, then side-slipped from beneath him and circled him, but his head was slumped in cockpit and he started in slow spin. Followed him down and gave him a couple more short bursts. As he went into the clouds saw him turn that orange red. Rest of flight nowhere to be seen so came below to see where I was. Came out in time to see my courteous friend hit a field just behind our trenches. Picked up rest of flight mixing up with Huns. Could only spot two of our planes.

9

Joined them and started to pick on Huns when they suddenly turned tail and ran for home. Quite low and as I levelled off saw Tommies waving their appreciation. On landing home found no one who had seen mine go down, felt sick. One had been shot down by Chilly and crashed other side of lines, confirmed by rest of flight. Got busy on phone while I went and changed into my mechanic's suit, ... , and went to overlook old "RIP," hit in more places than I care to think about, although nothing very serious. Up again after lunch and spotted two-seater circling over lines, our archie doing everything but hit it. Cautiously got the fellow spotted and crept up to him below clouds, using mist as screen. Didn't see us and when were almost over him went down on him. Almost immediately enveloped in myriad Huns and when about twenty-five yelping Huns sprinkle themselves around you not so comfortable—discretion would appear to be better part of valour, although not perhaps according to A.R. Decidedly more healthy. Our "retreat" masterpiece, all got away. Have queer feeling to-night, seems kind of rotten to have killed a chap who had waved and smiled at you, no personal reason for blowing him up, fellow like myself. Seems kind of damned silly and senseless. Deliberately killing someone you'd probably drink with and find pretty decent chap under other circumstances. Gets me under the skin. Bloody futile, all this. Spite of everything can't get lasting war lust into my blood—feel

10

ashamed of reaction, not the thing. Believe other chaps feel same way too, only how the devil could one admit that one feels sorry or fed up about it? All beastly futile anyhow, where's it all leading to? Always found Germans pretty decent chaps before war, can't think otherwise even now, damn it, and spirit shows, in their Flying Corps anyhow. Seen several instances of *esprit de corps* between flying forces. All seems bloody futile. Silly ass to think about it at all, better ginger oneself up instead of brooding, does no good, weakens one. Only wait until this filthy mess is over, and if I come through, damned unlikely unless it's soon, I won't half preach pacificism— let myself go for all I'm worth. Couldn't quite do it now, one has to stick to certain ethics now that the war is on, but only wait, I'll know what I'm talking about after the war, bet there'll be thousands of the same kind. Oh, well, what's the use, we won't get that far—be where the good niggers go by then, no two ways about it. Read pacifist speech in paper other day—"sacrifice of youth on altar to gods of Whitehall and the Wilhelmstrasse. . ." Damned right, but what can you do when it's on? Got to see it through, and Germans do think they're God Almighty. Can't allow that, certainly, but could think of better ways of putting them where they belong than this—anyhow Junkers should be first in field of battle, not the one's who have had no fun in life yet, who don't give any more of a damn for Imperialism than I do. Bet if Powers-that-Be had to lead into battle there'd be no

11

wars! Bright idea for election campaign. Oh, well, what's the use—we're in it and have to stick it out, no use grousing or even philosophizing. . . . . . . However, we shall see what we shall see, and to hell with being sorry about anything, better get going. Fun to see it through and what peace brings. Be pretty good feeling to laze the days away without sound of strafing from all directions. Almost forgotten what peace times were like, seem so long ago, lived so many lifetimes since. Can't imagine any other life, somehow. Anyhow, all things come to him who waits, most of us finish up with a cross over us, so what's the use of trying to imagine anything else.

SATURDAY. Waxed pretty loquacious last night—won't try that brand again. Must be sickening for something! Like to tear it out but will keep it in to laugh at, can't imagine myself writing all that in a sober mood. That's what drink does for one! Nothing exciting today.

SUNDAY. Sky full of black crosses. Toss up which to tackle. Didn't wait for them to do choosing, tore into them. Got above one flight and must have been at least fifteen in patrol. Dived on them and kept going. One left patrol and tootled back to his lines, rest tried to follow us. Tried same stunt, afternoon, and bit off more than could comfortably chew. Got away with skins intact. —Flight lost one of their men. . . . . . . Good pilot, too. Don't know what became of him, no one saw him disappear. We have to pay for our sport.

MONDAY. Splendid day! Two more out of it, Hendy, our flight, will live on German rations for rest of war and Lanky Mat will adorn hospital in Blighty for some time. Old Hendy must have got his engine hit as he landed well behind German lines, turned over and crawled out. Had time to burn his bus before Hun infantry took him over. Seemed unhurt. Damned lucky, I say. Lanky Mat managed to get back to our lines on one cylinder. . . . . . . Stout fellow, could easily have given up ghost, state he was in.

TUESDAY. Orders to nurse B.E., photographic work, watched hen to shoo Huns away, and they came, they saw, and what a scrap. Picked out what I took to be a novice, big mistake. Sparred a bit and he suddenly left me, next thing I knew he was diving on B.E. Went down after him but he twisted out of my way and gave me burst from just behind in fuselage. Fortunately observer in B.E. good shot, pilot no dud either, so they got away. No casualties on ours. One of B. Flight shot a Hun, seen to crash behind German lines.

WEDNESDAY. Had to rout out lot of Hun infantry behind —— proving too much of sore thumb for our infantry. Found them alright and they welcomed us with their warmest kind of hospitality. Circled and dived and picked out nests, and as they popped at me got them in the ring sight. Fascinating to watch them topple over. Ideal way to kill, in my opinion. No close contact with your victim, no blood, or shrieks or distorted looks of frenzied pain. Delightfully impersonal. All serene to-night.

THURSDAY. . . . . . . Air has a smell of freshness about it. Watched an old Frenchwoman and a little girl working in a field a couple of hundred yards to the north of us. Fit subject for Millet. Turned round to see C. Flight taxi-ing out for a patrol, subject for modern Detaille. Lovely war. Nothing of interest.

——DAY. Appears to be something unusual doing over near ——. Were kept busy. In my opinion every one of the crews of those old B.E.s should be given an M.C. even before they take off the first time over the lines. Were snooping around and we flew over them in case scouts should appear on scene. Funny what queer ideas come in one's mind when flying over the lines, archie all the time doing his damnedest to blow

14

you out of the sky. Always think of skinny old hen going about her farm duties whenever I see a quirk at work. Saw one Hun patrol high to the east but the B.E. apparently had done her work and was buzzing off so we did likewise. Rumours that. . . . . . Like all rumours of this war, never know when to believe them. If you do they are false, if you don't they are more likely to be true. Anyhow, if we do . . . . . . know it will be to do some hot work. But why think about it. Life is too short, out here any way, to bother one's head about anything. Canada just came in, says he feels homesick in this weather. Poor devil, thousands of miles from home. Anyhow, if he gets pipped old Peter will get a good pianist for the heavenly choir or orchestra. Is now playing Chopin. An hour ago he was careening through the sky.

FRIDAY. Coming in this afternoon saw what looked like a wrecked plane in some tree tops. Signalled to Chilly and pointed down to wreck. Went down to look at it more closely. Rest followed me, however, all trying to see what it was. Almost unrecognisable, such a wreck, but may be one of our two-seaters. Noted location on map for further investigation.

SUNDAY. Wangled afternoon off and went over to

—— to look at crash saw the other day. Managed to find it after much chasing around. Hun two-seater. Pilot and obs. buried by Tommies, they said. According to old Frenchman living near it had been there over a week. Tried to get Iron Crosses off wing but too torn up by branches. Tommies had looted thing properly and guns had been won. Was about to climb down when spotted something shining just forward of rear cockpit, nearly broke my neck getting it. Was a camera, strange looking contraption, cylindrical in shape. Badly dented. Heavy thing. Showed it to Jock who said lens by some miracle seems alright, and shutter is fastest he has ever seen. All excited about it, wanted to buy it, but I need a toy so think I'll hang on to it. Lens at least will come in handy if ever we get cooties, good magnifier. Had a film roll in it but back was smashed and film ruined. Interesting to know what was on it but all bashed in. Jock says we ought to repair it and use it up in the air, but I'm not a Siamese twin with four hands—besides, it weighs about ten pounds. Obviously the Germans were using it for some photographic purpose, and it's up to our combined brains to find a use ourselves for such a gift from the gods.

MONDAY. Pluvius, or whatever the honourable gentleman's name was who was O.C. rain for the Olympians, was active to-day and we had a little rest.

TUESDAY. If ever a prize is offered for the biggest ass in the R.F.C. I shall get it. Probably will be awarded posthumously and I shan't be able to join in the laugh. Got in a cloud mix-up this afternoon, visibility rotten anyway, and when I tumbled out of them looked around for the flight which appeared to be just ahead. Tore after them. They were flying in the lower part of the clouds almost concealed by the mist, and as it was bumpy was busy flying, not paying much attention to anything but catching up with them. Got my position again and was tootling along when I happened to look across at the bus flying opposite me. I was flying along with a Hun patrol! He seemed as surprised as I was and we stared at each other blankly for a few seconds. My brain then started functioning and I quickly turned and climbed up into the protection of the clouds and that was the last I saw of that patrol! True, Albatros somewhat like Nieup, and it was misty—only excuse I can offer. Hesitated to tell them in mess to-night, but did and had to stand champagne as result. Lesson cost me quids.

WEDNESDAY. Rotten flying so hung around mess. Rags brought ground glass out from —— for us and of course I had to crack one corner off cutting it to fit. Can see through camera now and Jock says it's remarkable lens, take good pictures. Talked a lot about focal

17

length and all that sort of stuff, Greek to me, but corner of hangar in focus and poplars along road to . . . . . . Odd size, four and eleven-sixteenths by little over three and a half. Jock suggests I fit a five by four rack in it and fasten it to the bus in some way and take pictures with it while up. He's great at making suggestions but doesn't wait to tell you how to go about it.

THURSDAY. Foggy. Spent day trying to devise some way to use camera while flying. Jock dashed over to . . . . . . several packs of plates, chemicals, etc. Takes a bit more thinking out than at first imagined. Canada just came in and showed me a letter from Fitts (my fitter):

> "My pilot is a bit of a kid
> and yesterday he blame near
> come to joining the Hun Flying
> Corps flying along thinking
> of his dinner and found himself
> flying along with the Hun
> squadron. Came home looking
> kind of sceared but he can fight
> when he is not asleep and me and
> Riggs is proud of him.
> Wen you go to Church on Sunday
> Mary put in a prayer for him along
> of me."

Now I simply have to justify my old Fitt's opinion of me. Tender from —— just blown in with almost everyone tight.

——DAY. Holly missing. First thing we ran into over the lines was D.F.W. No choice but to spoil his show. Watched few minutes, spied Albatros scouts higher up apparently watching gentle little lamb. They were above clouds so we tackled two-seater just as a cloud obscured him from his friends above. Can't understand such colossal stupidity but we took advantage of it. Chilly got Jerry just as Huns upstairs tore into us. Ripped into each other and soon found ourselves up against good crew. Heard well-known sound behind me as Hun put short burst past my ears. Slipped out of it and got another from somebody else in right wing. Beautiful shot, compact and very much to point. What happened next few minutes don't know. Split-arsed around, saw one of ours go down and break up, and we had come within 1,000 feet of the ground. Another on my tail and pulled up to see him beside me. Both hung there, engines full on, staring. Fell away and I turned. Some distance away rest were fighting off more Huns, could see they were trying to get back to our lines. . . . . . . Left us mile or so this side of our lines. Joined flight, saw one of Chilly's wires broken, ends trailing back. Pluckily he kept on and landed. Must have been Holly who broke up.

——DAY. Queer going up this morning without Holly. One day here, next day God knows where. Wonder who will be next. Nothing to report. Working on new toy.

SUNDAY. Tried to get balloon to-day but we failed. They must have some jolly powerful engines the way they wind them down. Huns upstairs were apparently delegated to watch it and as soon as we got near tore down into us and kept us busy. Bag pulled down, though. New man to-day in Holly's place, if such thing possible. Nice chap, hope he lasts. We carry on for long time without any casualties, get to know each other, then biffo, one after another goes, empty chairs night after night, new faces in mess, and so it goes. Helped him fix his bus, sight guns, gave him few tips. Holly evidently gone for good.

MONDAY. Huns starting some sort of activity, we kept busy shepherding B.E.'s and trying to prevent Hun photographic planes from coming over the lines. Am getting pretty good at spotting two-seaters. Have

studied their blind spots, soon be expert on them . . . . . .
two-seaters have observer who . . . . is far more
valuable man than we shall ever be. He must have knowledge of every branch of military activity to-day, and
that knowledge can't be obtained in ten hours or so of
instruction. His trained eye can see things of vital im-
portance which would escape the eye of the average
scout pilot. . . . . . . , ... observer is due
plenty of kudos, patiently stands by his gun in rear cockpit and gathers information so vital to the High Com-
mand, and gets very little attention from anyone for
doing so. Least of all must we forget the Hun ob-
servers. To exterminate them is my ambition, they play
the devil with us. No actual fights to-day but plenty
of planes in the air. Took Ham up for Cook's tour
after tea.

TUESDAY. Heaven sent rest to-day. Find it takes
longer to make gadgets than to draw plans for them.
Jock is washout as mechanic but old Fitts (fitter) is priceless, patient and makes many good suggestions. Twigged
my ideas quickly and great help. Had Riggs (rigger)
helping to rig up dark room behind our hangar but suddenly realised idea no good. Have to think of some other
place for dark room, everyone too curious.

WEDNESDAY. Clear day, hard work. Saw three two-seaters, after them full of confidence. Disappointed—crafty trio. Couldn't get burst into them, try as we did. Must have been good as even Chilly failed to get a pot in. And I was beginning to imagine myself good two-seater expert! Camera ready to try out now. Have had to suspend it under wing just beyond arc of prop. Found that when I tried to snap it through the prop always managed to get prop. blurred in. Have swung it so that it will hang level except on a vertical bank, and have fixed a Bowden control so that when I press the gun trigger the pressure on the wire will operate shutter. Streamlined the back and removed everything unnecessary. Looks like a small bomb. So when I am sitting on a Boche's tail ought to get snap of beggar same instant I put burst into his hide. Now the thing to do is to be sure and put plenty of salt on his tail and then pop him!

FRIDAY. Got a bullet through my rudder and some through my wings to-day. "RIP" got worst of it as usual. Fair fight, other fellow better pilot, that's all. No excuse for myself. Thank God still here. Managed to get away from him and safely home. Chilly brought one down with his first burst. Went down full engine on and wings came off. Had camera on and Jock developed plate to-night after dark, plate unexposed! Test on ground evidently not same as in air. Have carefully checked everything and can only think wind pressure on lever where Bowden connects with camera prevents it from operating in some way. Damned disappointing after all our brain fag over it. Am having Fitts make piece of metal as shield over it.

SATURDAY. Ripples of splash other day being felt in our sector now. Had to do with a lot of them to-day. Detest big fights, energy all taken up in avoiding collisions with careless pilots. One error is one too many, no second chance here. Got away from them with assistance of Pups. Got picture at last, but instead of Hun I shot at got a lovely picture of dear old Chilly flying peacefully along. I would forget something! High when we spotted Huns and I warmed the gun. When I did get a chance to pot one I thought I'd get a picture of it— according to my theory. Could hardly wait for it to get dark to-night for Jock to develop it. Anyhow, it's good, but not what we want. Proves that thing works. Am thinking out a method whereby I can operate shutter only on d.b. and not on t.b.

MONDAY. Watched some tanks for a while to-day. Those mastodons of mud certainly are funny looking things from the air. Must play hell with the Boche.

Coming in to land saw two staff cars on tarmac. Came bumping in like two-hour solo—brass hats got in my eyes and blinded me! Anyhow didn't break anything, but to complete things who should be in the group of gilded gods but the Sphinx. Tried to avoid showing myself at such unpropitious moment by slipping into hangar other side of bus, but Woolly saw me and hailed me before the birds of paradise for exhibition. Hoped Sphinx wouldn't remember me, but he did. Apparently change of climate has cured his liver, for he was quite chatty. Graciously congratulated me on my modest success. Wished me more luck.

TUESDAY. Solved difficulty of exposing camera when warm gun by having Fitts put extension on trigger to be used when I warm gun and not operate camera shutter, and have had another trigger made for camera Bowden next to gun trigger. No danger of my gloved paws pressing wrong place on it. Can hardly wait to try it out.

SUNDAY. Success at last. Got ripping snap. Had hot scrap this afternoon but all back. Energetic tribe of Huns who knew their business joined our patrol and result lively scrap. Huns knew every trick in the whole bag, and still had some new ones. Picked on Ham who gave them all he had and flew like the devil. He put up wonderful fight and got a cheer from us as he tumbled out of his bus on the tarmac, his face all grimed. His bus riddled, wonder it held together, but he is fully fledged now. My part nothing to write home about, got jamb at very beginning of business, couldn't clear it. Thought of clearing out of it but decided on bit of bluffing. Great what it will do at times, though nerve racking. Chilly pretty bucked when heard had stuck it out with jammed gun. Mother's good boy! Picture drying now, Hun below Nieup. is the one I tried to pot in the belly. Don't know who is in Nieup. Jock is bucked too, and wants to take camera up himself, when he is flying different time to me. Is having trigger and mount made now to fit on his bus.

MONDAY. Got Ham out of tangle this afternoon, all here. Mixed up with Halberstadts and suddenly saw two of them away off making one of our flight turn himself inside out. Slipped over and riddled one of them just as he was about to pip Ham. The sudden shock of getting burst in the region of his square head evidently changed his mind for he turned and ran home as fast as he could. Didn't follow as the other was still in the offing. But he turned tail also. Soon after spotted two-seater and went after it, but he saw us first and his engine was

25

"Hun below Nieup."

good. Got snap but it shows only part of Hun's tail, useless. Missed that shot properly.

TUESDAY. . . . . . . Suppose we are going to make a push and gain few feet of shell-torn mud and acclaim a victory. Matter of fact, if we have to wait for victory until Hun is pushed back inch by inch to the Rhine shall be getting my beard tangled up in prop. Nothing of interest to-day, mess intact.

WEDNESDAY. . . . . . Kept busy all day making things interesting other side of the lines. From what I hear will have heavenly time of it soon, can well believe it as Fritz in truculent mood. Oh, well, when the bullet with my name engraved on it comes along I shall get it, so what's the use. No use crossing bridges before come to them. Have to work out new dark room—try portable one under circumstances. Fold it up when we move, tie it with ribbon and bye-bye.

THURSDAY. Eye opener of a battle to-day. Thought —— pretty bloody but this one got them all beaten that I've seen. They must have blown the German trenches into splinters with mines, but you can hardly see anything because of dense smoke. Hell has broken loose, and if there are any Huns alive in that shelled area must be mental and physical wrecks. Up all day taking turns to keep the sky clear of Huns, and playing hell with the troops. Tanks everywhere. Thank God we have at last beaten Hun at his own game. Two missing, one C. Flight and one B. Flight. We escaped by some miracle. B. Flight got a Hun, however, to make up for it.

FRIDAY. Battle still raging on ground and plenty of it up in air. Huns sending up everything with an engine and wings. And they fight. Plucky devils. Awfully hot row. Jock sent one down out of control and is well over the eight now, celebrating . . . . Canada at piano now. Great lad.

SATURDAY. Easier to-day. Had bottom flight however this afternoon and hot time from infantry. Shot up several batches of them well behind lines. No one down or missing, all in good mood spite of heat. Only cool place upstairs. Jock and I busy on portable dark room, hope to have it finished to-morrow.

SUNDAY. Went into —— for binge this evening. Met C—— and R——. R—— expecting leave soon as this show is over. Lucky dog. C—— out on Bristols, awfully bucked about them, says he flies them like a scout and observer takes shot when he gets a chance. Am having a bit of insomnia. Tired, can't sleep.

MONDAY. Dark room finished, absolute waste of time! Light comes in through joins and what not. Useless. Damned bloody nuisance. Spent hours sticking up leaks of light, and as soon as one was fixed another broke loose. Another thing, too conspicuous. Have to stick to waiting until dark and doing it in hut, but must work out some other method for dark room, hut not very workable.

TUESDAY. . . . . . . Waiting for Jock, celebrating events of eventful day. Going into —— to make night of it. Worth it. Have to send for some sort of decoration right away! Got a Hun, saved a Bristol, got a bloody good picture all at same time. Ain't I smart? And if saving your skin counts for anything, which it does with me, think had better add bar to it. Picture priceless. Got chaperoning job. Tommie, Tubby and I had to keep eye on Bristol taking usual photographs of German residential sections, but from what I have heard of the Bristol Fighters those boys are well able to take care of themselves. Should Fates have ordained me to have been a sausage merchant should hate to attack one

"He got under tail of one of them"

"At about 8,000"

of them if they had a half way experienced crew. After shepherding for about ten minutes hell broke loose around us from nowhere. Albatrosses went at that Bristol like pack hungry wolves. Suddenly spotted Hun coming up under tail of Bristol and just as he was starting to open up spattered him generously. All over so damned quickly that takes more time to tell it than it happened. Hung on his prop for second then saw him flop over from stall and go down. Then he lit up. Why the devil can't some clever mind at home—where they all are—design a non-inflammable petrol tank? While it was going down was thinking to myself what a clever fellow I was (sic) and didn't notice another Albatros close to me, and before I knew it was peppered good and proper for my careless-ness. Kicked her hard over in a second, but got holes in my empennage, and my ego thoroughly deflated. If that Fritz had been as good a shot as some of his brothers—oh, what a death for a hero! Jock took up camera later and says they ran into Huns over —— at about 8,000. He got under tail of one of them as they dodged, and peppered him in his rear. Didn't get it, he says, as saw it turn and go down after one of our buses. From snap looks as if he started to shoot too soon.

FRIDAY. Back in the fold, and somehow feel glad. "RIP" waiting for me, and went up first patrol this

"Just as he left the burning plane"

morning and gave her morning bath in nice fluffy clouds. Emerged all freshened up in the sun. Some dachshunds were also performing their aerial ablutions and we had to pass time of day with them. Result—nothing. Well, one's eye is not always true, so can be excused. Finished patrol, after Huns slipped away, in peace, and came in for breakfast. Didn't have camera with me, sorry, as I might have got snap. Jock had it with him and didn't want to wake him up to get it. When I got in last night he was in ——, so didn't see him until this morning. Had two snaps which he got while I was away, one a corker, Albatros going down in flames and pilot jumping out. Unbelievable luck to get a picture like that. Dirty dog never kept notes of things, but of the burning one he said they ran into some Huns and Bristols and when they came into it, it was almost over. A Hun went down under control and Jock nosed after it to get it. Then saw it was on fire and followed it down, watching pilot struggle to bring it all the way down by sideslipping first on one side until that side was nearly burnt away then turning the other side down. Heat must have been terrific. Noticed pilot trying to jump out. He was done for anyway and Jock decided to give him a burst to end his agony, but as he was about to shoot him Hun pulled plane up into a stall and jumped. Camera caught him just as he left the burning plane which went fluttering down, mass of flames. Ghastly picture. Gives one creeps. Worse than seeing actual thing happen.

33

"Beautiful example of correct place to arrange your Hun before
shooting him"

Laddy and Bully have both been killed—took zest out of things a bit.

MONDAY. Now I know precisely how a fox feels with hounds at his heels. Chased almost home to-day by Hun Air Corps and haven't got my breath yet. Thanks to the tricky little Nieup. I am still here, for while Huns were faster they were not so good at dodging about landscape as I. Like a damn fool, lost rest of patrol climbing above some clouds, and while looking for them spotted pack of hungry Hun wolves coming at me. At first thought they were Nieups. although couldn't imagine how rest of flight could have climbed so high so quickly. Saw their little noses just in time. Those Albatrosses are speedy on the dive but I had the best of it when it came to split-arsing. Came out of clouds and headed for our lines, then began game of tag. Wasn't interested in getting Huns, in dead earnest about getting away from them. Five of them, so desertion was pardonable. Chased me over lines for several kilometres behind. Twisted and turned and duly came out without a scratch. What luck! Mess laughed when told them, but would rather provide them with laughter than a vacant chair any time.

FRIDAY. Jock, lucky beggar, got marvellous picture to-day, bang in centre of right sight. Beautiful ex-

35

ample of correct place to arrange your Hun before shooting him. Best picture yet, I think. Jock consented to stop long enough to tell me about it. "Let all the embryo pilots at —— study this picture and dream sweet dreams of doing likewise. Needless to say, the German exponent of the gentle art of aerial combat was not aware of my close proximity when I potted him or I should not have got such a good photograph, nor his scalp at the same time. Off in the distance a few hundred feet is one of those S.E.5s, trying to get on a Hun's tail or being chased, don't know which. Our *tête-à-tête* was a small one and not very exciting. Felt lazy so didn't try to scare up anything which might cost us extra effort, so tootled along quietly minding our own business, when batch of Huns saw us and, thinking we didn't see them flew along to our rear. Farrie waggled his wings that he saw them, too, and we slowly turned towards our own lines. Huns came after us, eight at least, then trouble began. Keeping clear of them spotted friend of photograph hovering on outside, so sneaked up behind him and let him have it. Went down, crashed in a field. Flight of S.E.s had joined in a few seconds after Huns came on us so Fritz didn't have much chance."

SATURDAY. Pat missing. Flew like hell to-day, plenty of air targets well as ground. Made most of it. Pat with us when we crossed lines so must be somewhere this side of them. Didn't worry much at first but beginning to now as it's late and still nothing been heard of him. May have had forced landing at some un-get-at-able spot and be tramping. Only one missing. Several brief contacts with Fritz to-day but nothing interesting. Did some ground strafing and made ourselves more unpopular with Hun infantry. Helped an old B.E. out of scrap this afternoon and she cackled away with her photographs like an old hen. Saw big scrap, morning, but all over by time we got there.

MONDAY. Rotten weather. Pat came in yesterday around lunch time. Landed this side of our lines, luckily, bus washout. Only bruise or two.

WEDNESDAY. Paid for our little holiday. Went well over lines and tackled anything that had wings and an Iron Cross. Our quirks were at it heroically. One of them great fighter. Was attacked by about six Huns and we were all in a mix-up, but instead of slipping out of it he stayed and fought it out. Stout fellow. Got one of the beggars before they slipped away. Both got more photographic duds to-day. They are all too blurry for some unknown reason. Had to chase Hun artillery bus out of sky but when got there naturally it had seen us coming and skipped. Instead of coming back to the drome we

"Lovely mix-up"

buzzed off and then came back again from the east and caught it on the job again. Honestly, this game over here is exactly like snaring rabbits sometimes. Best to see funny side of it! Hun scouts also appeared at same time with S.E.s higher up. Two-seater skipped again, but Pat managed to get one of the Albatros merchants in his ring sight and let him have a long burst. Doesn't know whether he got it or not, but saw it go down in tight spin. Jock couple over eight and is seducing Canada into playing the piano.

——DAY. Briddie and Cunny missing· Seem to have got caught in the entire Hun F.C. to-day. Wonder any of us here to-night. Cunny disappeared in middle of scrap with big Hun patrol. Were about 7,000 and Huns about 3,000 higher when we saw them. Patrol of French Spads even higher. For a while thought Spads didn't see Huns, but evidently did. Scrap lovely mix-up. Three holes in lower right wing. Huns skipped when more Spads came on scene from higher up. Can't understand why it is I snapped a Spad when should have got Hun. Only explanation we can think of is that pressure to shutter doesn't travel instantaneously. This gives delayed opening to shutter. Will have to go over it again. Remember distinctly pressing triggers when had Hun right in front of me, but got this instead. Worried about old Cunny as no one has idea where he is. Good scout.

B. Flight chap South African. Done for, as he broke up. Hope not in for repetition of last April. Have dismantled camera and am going over damned thing again to see where slow action is.

FRIDAY. . . . . . . Had our share of bad luck lately, can't do much worse. Up all day, hard at it. Air seemed full of planes, ours and theirs, and A.A. had great time. Chased two big two-seaters, but archie too good for us and followed the beggars until we had to slack off. German A.A. batteries are good, come too near for comfort. Shot up battery F.A. and put them out of action, for a while anyhow.

——DAY. (In bed). Better this morning, decent sleep last night first time for æons. Foot damned sore and aches, otherwise all serene, except "RIP" *non est*—feel as if my favourite dog or horse were dead. Loyal little devil but they got her in the end, as they will me. As it is I can't even get a Blighty, have to get myself bag of scratches and a sore foot, just enough to keep me here in this blasted bed for a few days, nothing to read, no one to talk to half the time, all I can do is write letters, work up my belated correspondence. Dud day so not losing much by being here. Old Turtle's mug is not seductive enough to make me want to stay in bed!

All the excitement I get is Rags after me for chess, damn him. Keep this diary by me and am busy writing in it every time hear his footstep. Only thing to write about is scrap other day, so am spinning it out to last until evening when the boys will be back again. Tackled three two-seaters Sunday afternoon, and those beggars knew their business. Tore around each other and tried to get one of them but he wasn't having any. Must have read me like a book for he banked suddenly and obs. got in good burst when I was momentarily helpless. Everything in cockpit seemed in splinters, engine coughed, I nosed down and managed to get across lines and land well behind them. Landed in shell hole, turned over, wriggled out of belt and crawled out of mess. Foot hurt like devil but could hobble a bit. Saw troops running towards me and walked to meet them, but hadn't gone 200 yards when two shells came over in quick succession and I ducked. When I looked back old "RIP" was blown to bits. Could have cried. Queer how attached one gets to one's bus, loyal little beggar, even at the end she brought me safely down and went out like a soldier should. Fitting end to a fighting plane, God bless her. Troops Canadians, priceless crowd. Hurried me to a dugout and bound up my foot with their own emergency bandages. Great boys. Fine looking crowd, too. No wonder Huns hate them, would rather be with them than against them myself. Huns shelling that part of line so had to stay there until dark, then taken to field dressing

41

station. They have the most priceless flow of mixed blasphemy and slang ever did hear, wish I could release it like that, and as glibly and expressively. Favourite expression "Goddam" and almighty expressive. Field dressing station renewed bandages, gave me shot anti-tetanus and shot me off to hospital. M.O. examined me, rebound bandage, kept me there all night, and only got here by skin of teeth, liked me so much wanted to keep me there. I don't think. Jibbed at being kept there, anyhow, said I would be well taken care of here, glad to get rid of me, I bet, so that's that. Promised to keep foot up few days and go back if I turn blue or green or anything! Much to my surprise Wing sent car for me. Must be rising in world. See big future for myself. Will have to use crutch for some time, M.O. said, but can fly, anyhow.

THURSDAY. Rags certainly has me at his mercy now. Wish were imaginative and could think up excuses and look busy when he comes around for chess. Bet I'll never look at a chess board as long as I live after this session. Don't mind playing chess, but he takes it so damned seriously. Begged off after two long games, bored to death. Going round on crutches, very much wounded soldier. Feel like hero in romance, but there are no romantic maidens around to see me. What a waste of good material. Went over camera gadgets, think I have overcome slow action trouble with shutter. Had Fitts

42

make some slight alterations in Bowden and in new trigger he had made for me. Also did some tinkering in dark room and have contrived whole developing paraphernalia in a collapsible box. Anyhow, thank God for that slow action trouble, wouldn't have had toy now otherwise.

FRIDAY. My new baby has arrived, and both doing well. Looked her over and she looks a ripper. Fitts and Riggs are working on her now and if foot goes along alright shall be up in her next week. Another "RIP." Shall stick to that name, it's a mascot. New man for A. Flight came in to-day, Ren, nice chap, public school man, long in leg and appears also long in knowledge of his business, was obs. on ——. Badly hit and transferred to scouts—out of frying pan into fire, if you ask me. Hazy this morning, no one up until late afternoon. Hated to see Flight go up without me. Sat on tarmac waiting for their return. New experience. What a feeling, waiting, then sound of returning planes, watching to see if all come back and counting. Relief when all there. Never noticed it before, never really thought about it. Hate to be sq. cdr. Jock had "bomb" with him, but no chance to use it— only one short brush, nothing doing.

SATURDAY. Jock blotto, half so myself. He had camera again to-day and when we developed snap

43

"Not the one I took the rattle from"

nearly bust with excitement. Corker. Got him to sketch out how he got it before he was too inarticulate! "Were treading blithely along above the clouds trying to keep cool when we spotted tag game to our left. Being in sporting mood we joined them, about eight Spads to five Huns, just as two Fritzies went down, one bursting into flames, other followed by a Spad into the clouds. Spads were getting the best of it and certainly didn't need any help, so we stayed outside for a few seconds to see what was what. Just as I was about to poke my nose into the melée an Albatros loomed slap bang into my ring sight. All happened so suddenly that I didn't have time to think twice and pipped him slap in the belly, forgetting for the moment that he was fair game for the Spad and that I had no business getting into a scrap like that for the Spad practically had him. Feel damned cheap about it. Thank God the Spad will never know who took his rattle from him. Hope he claims for the Hun for I won't. As the Hun went down I saw the Spad fall on him, giving him some more. Photo caught a second Spad, not the one I took the rattle from."

MONDAY. Up at last with my new "RIP." Leg still bothers me a bit and crutches are tiring. Drizzling now so no Huns overhead to-night, so, with bottle of cognac for companion, I sit me down to take a welcome rest. And, to increase the bells in the chime, got a Hun to-day,

"A perfect picture"

together with a perfect picture. Even Jock admits that it needs little retouching to make it work of art. The big boy skidding to one side of the picture is my scalp. Must take this in to show old Skipper. Will be certain to get tight. We seem to be taking tea with the Germans quite a lot lately in company with the Spad squadron, and they are welcome guests, to be sure. Lost Tubby somewhere to-day, no one saw him go down but so far this evening the Wing has heard nothing. Not seriously concerned yet as he has happy knack of pulling himself out of a bad hole and crawling home like a half-drowned cat. Jock has an idea for making the snaps more distinct. That chap is a born artist, never satisfied until he has achieved perfection.

TUESDAY. Tubby was down our side of the lines, heard late last night that he was coming home fast as side car could get him here, and arrived in due course wet to the skin and tight as a drum. After sticking around drome all day on account of fog, cleared towards evening and all went up. Jock and I tossed for camera and I won. And what a picture I got this time—"betterer and betterer." Ran into tangle of Spads and Albatrosses. We were right above the clouds and as soon as the Fritzies saw us they dived into clouds and were lost. Took a pot shot at one and missed, of course, but to my surprise, when Jock developed the plate found I'd got something

"Betterer and betterer"

pretty good. Plate is scratched in several places, but Jock says he can fix it up for me. Tried new stunt this time with camera angle, pointed God knows where, but result pleasing as London fog out here. Will experiment more and see what I get. If only I could devise some method of getting a film which would automatically move after each snap, what a lot we could get between us.

SATURDAY. It's a great life these days, what with one thing and another. Air alive with planes every time clear enough to fly, and believe we have Huns on run at last. Now that we are supplied with better planes he has a hard time keeping us from literally driving him from the sky. He creeps along in big patrols while we seem to come and go almost as we please. Missed my first shot and got no decent picture as result. Wing tip. Another throwout.

SUNDAY. Thunderstorm played hell with us this morning when we were on patrol over Hun lines. Threatening as we went over but fury of storm nearly ended patrol for good. Ren got lost and was not heard from until late this evening. Rain cut like hot needles in the face and could only fly blindly trusting that I was not going in wrong direction. Gusts knocked me all over place, compass seeming to spin in all directions. Kept her

49

nose up for height and unearthly darkness only relieved by flashes of lightning, furious thunderclaps. Hell let loose. Tried to climb above storm but was tossed about like piece of paper. Suddenly tremendous bluish light illuminated sky for second and within fifty feet of me was a Hun two-seater. Obs. sheltering his face, was facing me. Then blackness came over everything and deafening clap of thunder split the air. Evidently the Hun agreed with me—"to hell with everything only let me get on solid ground again." "RIP" held together and fighting every inch of the way we suddenly emerged from the storm. Found where I was after several minutes, throttled down and came home, and never has the old drome looked so cheery to me as it did to-night. Even the ruts gave me a comforting feeling! Worst storm was ever in flying.

WEDNESDAY. Tommie won a Vickers and gear from a crashed S.E. near —— and is having armourer sergeant sweat blood mounting and timing it. Sounds like a battery now. We are waiting for him to shoot his prop off.

SUNDAY. Bad weather last few days. Busy all day to-day. Kept watch over B.E. chaperoning old hen in spite of persistent attentions of Huns. Got fair photo in one brief brush but plane too far distant to be worth keeping. We're getting very "choosey" these days, throw out anything which is not up to scratch. One time would have thought the one I got to-day a pipper. What a lot of throw-outs we do get though. Find only ones worth keeping are those got on first contact when only few feet from Hun.

THURSDAY. Got stunning snap to-day, although pretty awful. Up this afternoon and after had been over lines about half hour saw scrap between Nieups. from —th Sq. and two-seaters. Turned into it and as we got near saw Hun burning up, Nieup. circling it. Hun scouts appeared just then and scrap became general. Noticed the Nieup. which was circling Hun in flames suddenly pull loop and just then one of the scouts dashed across my sights and I popped at him. Heard somebody's wing go and for second thought it was mine—what a feeling! Second later saw Nieup. going down in pieces. Suppose scout, which I pipped had hit him first when he was on top of loop, or he may have been badly hit and strain of loop broke plane up. Didn't see my Hun go down so don't know if I hit him or not. Jock developed plate this evening and result sort of hit us amidships. Pretty ghastly. Must have broken up at instant I pressed the trigger when popping the Hun. You can see the smoke of the burning Hun in lower corner. We got through to —th Sq. and inquired about their

"Must have broken up at instant I pressed the trigger"

losses to-day. Only lost one, new man. Needless to say, we didn't say we had photo of him cracking up. Wish to Heaven I could show it to them. Only thing can imagine is that if he was new man probably so excited at bagging Hun that forgot he was in France with war on and looped, fatal thing to do, never know where hit, in scrap.

FRIDAY. Worked like hell all day. Met up with big Hun patrol morning, kept above them until got sun behind us and then lammed into them. Outnumbered us three to one, but we took chance. Unfortunately they were all good fighters and we had our hands full. That was obvious at first contact. Missed everyone on first dive, and when we pulled up they were all on our necks. Then fight began. Hot stuff—too hot to be comfortable. "RIP" held together, luckily, and I threw her around cruelly, and we managed to get on the outside of the mess and tackled one of the Huns. Split-arsed around each other for few seconds trying to get on each other's tail, when another jumped on me. Pugnacious chap, flew damn well, knew his business. Got burst into puggy one which cooled his thirst somewhat, then quickly half-rolled and caught the other one but could only pop his tail. Near ground, and decided if didn't get one of them quickly they'd get me. Suddenly Nieup. flashed past me and from within few feet plugged puggy one good and

53

"Jock came down with good picture"

long. Other chap took hint, went down fast and away. Puggy one kept on flying in downward curve and saw him dive almost vertically, full engine on, into ground. Tubby got him, celebrated to-night. Only dark spot is plate—camera didn't even work—plate not even exposed! Confound. Can't get thing to work consistently, never know when it's going to let me down, miss a lot that way probably. This time, however, bullet broke Bowden, so can't grouse too much.

SATURDAY· Filthy day, carried on in spite. Tore into P.B.I. Chased two-seater out of sky, he had damned good engine, stuck fingers to nose at me, probably Eton boy! Jock came down with good picture. Says camera functioned beautifully. They spotted two-seater and went down on her before patrol could stop them. Little hazy and A.A. bursting all around them so suppose escort didn't see them at first. Tore down and obs. potted them. Pilot nosed home but they were too close and he and Farrie got good bursts into her. Feels good, even if he did get some holes through his bus. Couldn't wait to see what became of hen as Huns from upstairs were on them, playing hell. They got away, none missing. Damn good picture, I think.

SUNDAY. Feel in no mood to write to-night. Sick

"They got there first"

of war and everything connected with it. Like to stay blotto rest of time, beyond thinking. Found Huns this side of our lines this afternoon. Must have lost their bally way! Went at them, managed myself to get one of them away from rest, got burst into him as he was half-rolling away from me. Didn't put him out of commission so gave him another at close range. He faded out of mess just as his pals dived for their own lines. Could see way he was flying he was groggy. Came close up to him, he was flying towards our lines in long glide, engine turning slowly. Flew just behind him on his port side. Didn't pay any attention to me but kept getting lower and when he got within range of smoothish field seemed to pull himself together and landed, turning over. Circled awhile but he didn't get out, stuck in cockpit head down. Saw some of our men from heavies run over to where he was; lifted him out and laid him on ground. Apparently dead. Felt like bird of prey watching victim slowly die. Makes me sick. Finally got through on phone and took sidecar to where he had come down. Found place after lot of tearing across country. Battery officers showed me where they had buried him, cross up already. Gave me his watch, papers and other belongings, Iron Cross amongst them. Thought I might like them for souvenirs! Dinner with Battery, buzzed back. Said he was very young chap. Bloody sickening mess, whole thing, even if I did take on job of professional killer with my eyes open: gets me sometimes.

MONDAY. Fritz very busy these days, all we can do to keep them away from our lines. B.Es. and R.E.8s. being chased all over sky, do what we can to protect them but can't do impossible. Saw three R.E.8s. being kicked around by Hun two-seaters so we joined fracas and good old R.Es. didn't skip but stayed until we had chased Huns down to ground. Afternoon went up into Hun lines and shot up ——. Found several trains there full of troops and played merry hell with them. Just as we were leaving scouts came at us but we slipped away.

TUESDAY. Got all excited this morning, pressed wrong trigger and snapped shutter too soon but got good picture, even if it is a little blurry. Tommie, as usual, is in the limelight where he likes to be, and just between his wing tip and fin is Chilly. Got one of the D.Hs. as he was slipping away in a hurry into the clouds, with part of the pack of yelping wolves tickling his tail. We had been patrolling above the low clouds when spotted flight of D.Hs. staggering along with load of fresh eggs for starving Huns. Suddenly Chilly signalled "E.A." and we altered course to divert their attention to us and away from D.Hs. but Huns canny lot, kept well up and got into the sun. Then came down like winged bricks on bombers. We came down too, but they got there first and as D.Hs. broke up and dived into clouds we jumped on tails of Albatrosses. In second all

58

in damp fog, and when we came out below found Hun sitting on my tail, shooting steel through my wings. Do queer things when suddenly scared. Slammed stick over and to my surprise found grey belly in my sights and pressed trigger. Must have got burst in his bottom, dived for home like streak. D.Hs. split-arsing around in their clumsy way, but good lot of scrappers, and we kept at Huns like swarm of wasps. Saw one of them go down with black trail of smoke, then slipped under tail of another as he was peppering D.Hs. He came to in time to slip out of burst and we circled each other. Damned good pilot, determined to finish me off so could get at D.Hs. again but am not as clumsy as I seem to be, and kept him interested. Calmed down a bit when I accidentally put short burst into his tail again, and he flew more carefully. By this time had engaged all the Huns and next glance I got of D.Hs. they were couple of miles away, scuttling like hell into Hunland, complete with eggs. Bit of good work. After tearing around for some time saw another Hun spin into a field and then broke off and tree-hopped for home. Didn't follow as too low, came back to our lines. Just as we got over Hun trenches Tommie left us suddenly, saw him hold off and land carefully in shell-hole and arrange beautiful crash. Circled and watched him crawl out and he waved. Landed just behind —— and managed to phone through later, saying he was walking home in his bloody flying boots! Soaked through in storm and wet duds must weigh a ton! Take some of his fat off! Said machine-guns got him over trenches. Can imagine his state of mind when he gets in if he has to walk far. Fat, lazy beggar, crack pilot but no pedestrian. Sent side-car to fetch him, gave driver bottle of whisky to put spirit into old Tommie as he bumps his way home. Ham got the one in flames and Tommie the one in the field. Ham confirmed it. Cheery news for him when he gets back, bloody flying boots and all.

WEDNESDAY. Fritz fighting hard, we worked all day trench strafing and breaking up his attacks. If we had three times the planes we have think fight on ground would be different matter. Wonder if I shall see end of it all. Wonder if I'll ever fly over Berlin.

FRIDAY. Over to-day with usual message of love and good cheer for devil's darlings. One group to-day damned impudent, and instead of scattering when I dived on them, stood their ground and fired back at me. Have to admire their guts, but sort of annoyed me, so turned, and coming low skimmed the ground about six feet up and then heading straight at them pressed the trigger. Flatter trajectory caught them more easily and they toppled all over the place. Wind up for second as was afraid would miss some of them and they would be too stupid to duck, and was waiting that fractional part of second for my under-carriage to hit one. They ducked!

SATURDAY.   Jock got good snap to-day, about time, he said. He has had several scraps but until to-day only succeeded in getting tips of wings or planes so far away as to be mere specks on plate. In mix-up to-day with S.E.5s. from —th Squadron when he got chance to pot Hun. Doesn't think he got him, or even put bullet in his hide. But picture he got is ripper. Shows one of S.Es. diving on Hun's tail. Were right in clouds when they met the Huns, and aside from few spots is work of art. Dust and muck get over everything in dark room, even though we strain water and don't smoke and all that sort of thing. Jock is going to fix them up first opportunity.

SUNDAY.   Still alive to-day but can't imagine why or how. Had to go far over the lines as a feeble escort for some D.H.4s. Were ready to turn back when lot of E.A. came down on us and broke up little parade. Plucky bombers, heavy with eggs as they were, put up a great fight and gave back as much or more than the Huns gave them. Had tried a new angle for the camera pointing straight back and at the d.b. was smacking into a fat Hun with complacent smirk on my mug when—bang— a lovely burst in the engine. What a sickening sensation.

61

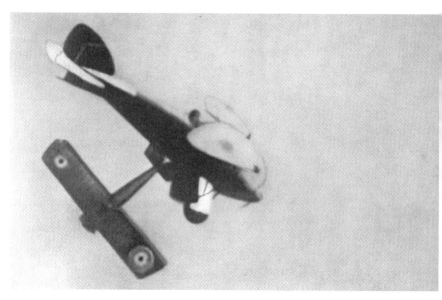

"Diving right across my ring-sight"

"Mix-up to-day with S.E.5s"

Miles over the Hun lines and 10,000 feet up. Engine dropped revs. until was just able to keep her up. Spun out of the fracas and prayed at the same time that the Huns wouldn't see me. Prayers unanswered, one of the blighters followed me down. But Tommie saw me and came down on that Fritz like a hawk. He got him at the first burst and I flattened out and headed home. Talk about slow torture! Flying over Hunland with a dud engine coughing and barking, and losing height every minute, watching the sky for Hun planes and getting archied every minute, then spotting some of the buggers who fortunately don't see you, is not an ideal way to spend half an hour. Got home with couple of hundred feet to spare and landed without crashing. Never realised how really beautiful the old drome was until to-day. Bus not a washout. Miracle tank not touched. What an amount of punishment a bus will stand at times, and again what a lot of damage only one bullet will cause. Jock couldn't find any more grey hairs in my head however. With lovely snap, feeling better. Think Hun in centre of picture must be chap who pipped me, as I was pressing trigger when got hit. Don't know who is in Nieup. One of lumbering bombers on top. Tommie says D.Hs. got away and kept on into Hunland afterwards. Afraid "RIP" out of commission for few days, but hope not. Hard at it in hangar, sergeant says I might be able to take her up day after to-morrow.

MONDAY. Stood on tarmac to-day watching my flight take off without me. Chilly's little fox terrier was there with me. That little beggar has more sense than the average human being. Sat on his haunches and wouldn't be coaxed away until flight came back. Did not even cock his ears when B. Flight came in a little while after ours had taken off, but when A. Flight returned he watched each plane as it landed and when Chilly climbed out of his bus he jumped all over him. Some bishop, asked if dogs had souls, said he couldn't imagine a Heaven without dogs. Damned right. Best little friends in the world. Going into —— to relieve monotony to-night.

TUESDAY. A Hun at last! About time, too. Plenty of them about full of fight. One minute sky is clear, next minute littered with black crosses and cockades. Never know when you're going to hear crackle behind your ear. Except for odd more or less easy day, almost as bad as —— lately. Tubby got one out of control, but we couldn't confirm as we didn't see it crash. Spotted big fight between Spads and Albatrosses this morning when we crossed lines. Saw one go down, then break up, followed second later by Spad in flames. Sight. Bet never knew what hit him. Everyone tired to-night, mess fairly quiet. The Bard sprawled in armchair, dreaming of his braes, Farrie and some others playing bridge, Woolly changing pins on map. And few hours ago everyone over lines fighting like mad. Queer life. Canada just came in and is playing piano.

WEDNESDAY. Jock got Hun down out of control but wasn't able to see it hit ground and no one else saw it. Too bad. Halberstadt. Wants to go over and find crash, if any, but he is positive there is, then dive and take photo of it. Not bad idea.

FRIDAY. Over to-day. No scraps. Jock found his crash. Almost ruined plate hurrying development, but it is positive proof beyond all doubt, so has put in for it. No end bucked at photo, said was worth all time he has spent on the thing helping me, to get that one photo.

SATURDAY. Went after two two-seaters this evening which Camels were trying to get. Two-seaters seemed to be faster and were not going to be shot down as easily as Camels hoped. We were a little higher and came down on two-seaters in endeavour to head them away from their lines. Put several short bursts in their general direction but was absolute dud to-day.

MONDAY. Woke up this morning to heavenly music

of rain on the roof. Angels can play their harps all they like, give me the gentle patter of the raindrops on the roof when that roof happens to be a hut in France with a war on and myself a sky fighter! Rolled over and slept on. Too often wake up in sweat to find I am not falling into space or going down in flames after all. Let all agonies be dreams as long as an occasional victory is a reality! Whole squadron lunched together for a change, cheery party, ante-room like London club. Got licked at chess again by Rags. Just washed out, 3 p.m. Going into —— for dinner. Wine, women, and song seem to be only pastime these days, and songs are seldom heard.

TUESDAY. Met Storky —— in officers' club in —— last night, left him tight as a tick. Still understudying Atlas and piloting R.E.8s. Don't blame him for trying to drown his sorrows with a job like that. Met Major M—— having dinner with charming little lady of about seventeen, ambulance driver. M—— keeping eye on her morals amidst all these bad boys. Asked me to join them, needed no coaxing. Caught last tender skin of teeth. Dud day to-day, so Jock proceeded to elaborate on his idea for making "works of art" out of our "illegitimate babies." Result, piled into tender for ——. At least hope we can take out squadron insignia markings more neatly than we have been able to up to now. . . . . . . Had some enlargements made. Had to lose quite a lot from some of plates to straighten them out, but Jock said it was necessary as otherwise you would have to twist your neck to look at them if ever the time comes when we can hang them up in our peaceful homes for our wives, kith and kindred for to see and admire! Long after dinner when we finished. Dined in cosy little estaminet, good food and wine. Then dashed back to drome. Myself would prefer to leave pictures as they are, just scratch out identifying markings, but Jock so enthusiastic, and such damned good fellow, helped me no end, so am not saying anything. Excuse for me to go into —— and fetch them to-morrow. Like to see little kid again.

WEDNESDAY. Spent most of day with pencil and rubber covering up all tell-tale markings, etc., on snaps. Hope it's dud again to-morrow so can finish job. Beastly work, tedious, but rather fun making struts plainer and shading in indistinct planes, but straightening some of the pictures has made some of the planes seem nearer than they really are. Jock spoiled one by getting too much paint on and it kept smearing all over place. Have to get another enlargement to work on.

FRIDAY. All up when it cleared, sky littered with planes. Didn't make contact with any E.A but saw scrap. Got there when all over. Finished all pictures and Jock's idea certainly makes them clearer. Have had to lose a lot in levelling them up. Take them to —— first opportunity and get him to make copies for us. All numbers and squadron markings out, so no one can identify squadrons. All serene.

SATURDAY. New chap for B. Flight. Bit old for flying, seems, but never can tell fighting pilot from his years or lack of them. If only we could combine experience of years with nerve and gusto of eighteen—oh, what a fighting force! Name is Buck. Has Kip's bunk. Stayed awhile chatting while he unpacked his kit. Pulled photograph out and put it beside his mirror. Blew his nose and fumbled in his kit-bag a bit. I wandered to door and called for a couple of drinks to celebrate his inauguration into fold. Chatted over them, told me he had married just before coming out to us. Been out before with ——, didn't feel so cheery about coming out this time, under circumstances. Don't blame him. Must be hell to leave new wife, knowing damn well chances are you will never see each other again. Can't make up my mind whether it's right or wrong to get hitched up to somebody you care for these days, although it doesn't concern me. Like to have all that's coming to me before I go west. One bad break sort of sours one.

SUNDAY. Rotten weather continues. Getting fed up with it. Relief from flying all right, but can have even more than you want of that, with so few other diversions. Decent sort of padre held services for troops in rest near us, invited us to attend. Pleaded that we had to stand by in case of break in weather. Thin excuse, he saw through it, but smiled quite decently. Seems good sport. Understanding sort of bloke. Like him because he tried none of usual arguments of persuasion. All seems so senseless and illogical to pray to God, then drop the Bible and fly at each other's throats. Got to be sort of consistent somehow. Can't sit through that sort of thing until I can get another sort of perspective on life.

——DAY. Up this afternoon and found front lines still there, as well as A.A. artists marring Heavens with their black smudges. Had camera on in fond hope of getting good snap as well as Hun's scalp, nothing doing. Getting used to bus now and find she is handy as well as fast. Have to watch her on landing. Poor old Bard washed his under-carriage off landing this evening. Only his feelings hurt.

WEDNESDAY. Perfect picture but would, of course, be a mess. Bucked at getting another one. Wouldn't staff at —— like to hang this in their ante-room as

69

"Good picture to-day"

example of a perfect O.K., and it was—saw poor devil start to smoke. Rather heavy ground mist to-day, but over twice, early morning when got good picture, and this evening when I got another one. Ordered up for some unknown reason to assist Camels entertain bevy of Albatros beauties, but Camels, in my opinion, were well able to entertain their guests on their own. Someone must have stumbled on a paint factory near their aerodrome for the Huns are coming out in Joseph's coat of many colours. Some are quite works of art, look like tropical birds. One I pipped to-day had even painted his helmet to match ensemble. For some reason camera anchorage must have loosened as this picture is not as good as it might have been, but general plan pretty good. Got Hun as he was diving slap across my ring sight on to one of our flight. Must have riddled him amidships. In the do this evening missed them and scrap only lasted few seconds. Were off quick as they came. Photo too blurry. Chuckout.

FRIDAY. No improvement in sky so did one short patrol and came back, washing out after tea. Went into —— and spent evening with ——. Too many trips there lately. Must stick to my philosophy of not taking anything seriously these days. She had to go on duty later in evening, so came home early.

71

SUNDAY. Got orders to clear out stubborn machine-gun nests, and had to go over for them. Found them soon enough, and they gave us back all we handed them with interest. Those boys certainly know how to shoot. Have had several patches put on "RIP" as result, but was lucky not to get permanent patch of ground for myself. All here.

MONDAY. After w.o. went with Canada across to infantry rest camp. Good lot of chaps there, ——. Had tea with them. One of them came from —— where —— lives. Knew her family, but said she was a school kid who always insisted on having her hair cut like a boy when he last saw her, couldn't believe she was out here. Just like her, what I like about her is that she has no sickly femininity, too young, I suppose. She'll learn! Maybe no sisters has something to do with it.

WEDNESDAY. Things are getting hot. Good picture to-day but missed old Fritzie. The Skipper ordered us along old canal and then on over towards ——. Hadn't been there long when spotted Albatros scouts. Kept in sun long as possible, then dived on them. Their Archie spotted us through opening in clouds, but warned them too late as we were on them just as they bunched almost wing to wing before they scattered.

Missed mine but Ren pipped one and Huff also. They didn't put up any fight at all but scuttled away as fast as their engines would pull them. Chased my elusive friend but couldn't get him. When they got down on the carpet all slipped away towards home. However, did get pretty damned good picture which is some compensation. Ren's plane can be seen in upper right-hand corner. Huff is below, I think. Poor beggars, so sure they got their man, and when we saw them hedge-hop away intact knew they had been playing with us. Snap light struck, damn it.

THURSDAY. Buck gone west. Damn rotten luck, only out few days, three or four times over lines. I knew it was no good getting married. Jock back to-day. "London is like it used to be, the Strand's still there." Rotten day, had to do lot of trench strafing and generally making things miserable for the Hun.

FRIDAY. Canada gone. Of course that would happen. Just as soon as one gets attached to something, bang, it goes. A most excellent view of our "Christlike" attitude towards life these days can be obtained from a front line aeroplane. The inhabitants of this part of the world are especially qualified to bear witness of the loving kindness and fatherly care which "His" followers

73

"A good picture"

practise, in particular those whose homes are a mass of ruins and whose families have been blown to hell by "His" children from across the Rhine. Bloody logical, the best are snuffed out while the gentlemen at home are keeping their expensive and *indispensible* backsides warm in cushy jobs, protected and cherished according to those same "Christlike" doctrines. Canada, gentle little fellow with the soul of a Galahad, who cheered us up by his music—and his example—who vomited whenever he shot down a Hun, is pushing up daisies to-night because he played the game as we've all been brought up to play it. We are all out here, we don't know what for and we shall all peg out for no earthly reason except that we tried to play the game, no other reason. Only thing we can do is to peg away at our job and hope for the best, whether it's here or above or below, one of the three, so what's the odds. Got to see the thing through as best we can anyhow. Strange silence hangs over the place to-night.

TUESDAY. Jock got a good picture to-day. Albatros shown is blurred a bit but good of one of ours diving. Buried long burst in Hun. Went down like stone. Farrie and Sandy saw it crash.

WEDNESDAY. Had hopes of day off, but weather

"Good one of ours diving"

"Met Hun patrol"

cleared about lunch time and we went over. Just as well as got good snap. All felt in vindictive mood and when we met Hun patrol had no mercy on them. Fought them all the way from 12,000 feet to the ground, getting one of them. All here, thank gods. They slipped away from us and we hedge-hopped all the way back to our lines, emptying our guns on P.B.I. en route. No word from Canada so far, and hardly expect any. He's a gonner. All the best fellows seem to go.

THURSDAY. Canada alive. Best news for weeks. Everyone acted as if war were ended. German pilot dropped note over our lines, he is not hurt beyond bad shaking up and is at ——. Asked for toothbrush, razor, some clothes and all soap we could lay our hands on. Made up package, put in plenty of gaspers and also some for German squadron, with note of thanks to them for treating Canada so well. Drew lots as to who would fly it over to him and Mick won. As we "kissed him good-bye" made him promise not to land and stay over there. He hedge-hopped over front lines and came back without scratch. . . . . . . Dropped package, circled again and dropped second package of cigarettes for German squadron. One of officers picked it up and when he read label saluted and waved to Mick. Everyone seemed to be happy and Mick said he was tempted to land and have lunch with them. Wouldn't have been surprised if he had

"Got good snap"

done that very thing. Everyone full of pep to-night, like a cloud lifted from mess and celebrations rampant. Queer thing, sporting spirit which exists between the two fighting forces.

FRIDAY. Jock could hardly wait to get his togs off to-day when he came in. Had snap of Fokker Tripe. Both rushed to dark room, and as image slowly came up mutual brimstone remarks increased. All he had got was tip of its tail, saying, as it were, "Cheerio, old thing, better luck next time—perhaps." Jock broke plate into 100 pieces and we went off to drown our disappointment in Scotland's dew, as The Bard calls it.

TUESDAY. Promised Jock first call on camera until he got decent snap, to-day he came in with one. Orderly had nice fire burning, which is welcome to-night, and we are enjoying double whiskies and soda. Jock says they bumped into two-seater being coddled by V strutters, and feeling full of beans after dull days lately, tore into them. Good fight. He got long burst into two-seater which sent her scurrying home nose well down. Must have hit her sore spot. Doesn't know who S.E. belongs to on left of picture. Got portrait of V strutters at same time, family group, as 'twere. "German aviators showing their tails to the enemy." S.E. at left spoiling

".... family group as 'twere"

the picture as the ever-present bystander has to stick his mug into any group into which he is not invited. Good moon to-night—let's hope better weather omen, for hot time promised us shortly.

WEDNESDAY. Lough came back from leave to-day, having added a wife to his burdens. Another good pilot tripped up. Celebrated in grand style, Chilly's dog dressed up as bride with tablecloth and wreath sat next Lough at dinner. That dog damned good actor. Put Lough to bed biffed to the world. Mess in good form to-night, everybody happy.

THURSDAY. Another big push, did what we could to help along the good work by ground strafing. Shell smoke hung heavily over lines and mist thick in places. Had several brushes with E.A. which also were over low to see what they could do. Nobody down.

SATURDAY. Not exactly ideal flying weather but manage to go over in between rough spots and cheer up Huns with bombs and hot steel. Not awfully bucked about ground strafing in this rotten weather. Have a brain wave to place camera in fuselage just behind me

"A mix-up"

and pointing back and up enough to clear fin. Think I can do it.

WEDNESDAY. The Bard down, landed safely well behind lines, sure he is prisoner as they saw him burn plane after he landed. He would, if it was his last gesture in this life. Jock great luck to-day, hottest snap we've had yet, or could hope to get. Keeps tramping about whirling his arms, flight thinks he has D.T.'s and he's so excited hasn't even had a drink yet. C. Flight were ordered to keep a special watch over Bristol taking photos over ——. When they got there she was waiting and was soon on job. Not a Hun in sight so they climbed above her and watched, hoping for cushy job. Camels passed, dipped their wings and disappeared off to the south. Suddenly they spotted Huns heading for Bristol in long fast dive, went down and in second air was full of planes around that Bristol. Jock got fat Hun and gave him burst long and sweet. Wash from his prop gave him a bad bump which probably saved him from getting hit as another Hun swept past him shooting long burst. Jock can't describe what happened after first wild scramble, but they fought like dogs over bone, and bone was no dud fighter either. Says Bristol merchant could handle his bus beautifully as he manœuvred to get away from Huns. They tried to keep them away from Bristol, and got one that he is sure of, Farrie got that one in flames. Jock must have sent one he popped down out of control as it was a yellow one and he didn't see it any more. No one else saw it go down so he is unlucky. Bristol suddenly disappeared, he caught sight of it in distance heading for our lines. Afterwards Huns dived away and they didn't follow. Just before they left they saw The Bard go down but he was under control and made nice landing, but was east of our lines. Picture a ripper, hot stuff. No end bucked. Got it when they were in first close mix-up, and looking at it it's marvel no collisions. Moment later, Jock says, had spread out and fight was on. Mick is S.E. diving on top of picture. Jock says snap needs a little retouching to sharpen some of them, but not much. Personally I think it's wonderful as it is.

THURSDAY. Either a feast or a famine in the photographic line with us—I haven't had a snap worth keeping for ages. My turn with camera to-day and got good one. Spotted small formation at northern end of our patrol to-day peacefully tootling along southward. Sun was right for us as we were turning when I saw them, then noticed one lagging behind the rest. Engine trouble probably. Ground mist heavy, almost like fog, and Archie didn't bother us. Crept closer on straggler and all dropped on poor bugger. Just as we were on him pilot must have heard us as he looked back. But too late, second later he was riddled and fell down in slow spin, then smoked. Rest of his patrol turned and seeing six of us decided to seek lower and safer regions. Went down like bricks without wings. Followed but they risked tearing their wings off, and we left them to do it. Topping snap. Luckily had not changed position of camera and had it pointing straight ahead. No end bucked. Drew lots for his scalp and Tommie won. Get so many dud photos that am wild when get decent one. Nearly as good as a Hun. No one missing to-night.

FRIDAY. Rained to-day, generally miserable, but we went over. Least we can do is to help poor old infantry. Strafed Huns and prayed at same time that engine wouldn't let me down. Gas and H.E. shells splashed mud sky high and shell holes full of water. ——do was a hot affair but methinks this is no picnic. Fritz is stubborn, and while we didn't see one Hun plane to-day he will be back again with us to-morrow or day after. They can say what they like about the German pilot, but he is not a coward. Just has a grain or two of everyday common sense. Am inclined at times to think we could do with little more of that commodity. Bad storm came up this afternoon and had to fight our way back against filthy wind. Glad to be here in front of nice warm fire and pretend I'm at home. Still hard at it on my new idea and think I have solved it.

"Jock ... snapped a Hun as it was trying to shoot a burst into him"

MONDAY. Short scrap few hundred feet over Hun trenches this morning. No results. Those Fokker Tripes can turn around and split-arse on a sixpence. Camera drew blank. After tea had Fitts help with new mount in fuselage. Have got it, I think. Jock is going to rig his up that way, too.

TUESDAY. Jock got corking good snap to-day. Light ground mist, but otherwise good day for a change. Plenty of Huns came out to bask and C. Flight bumped into flock of them. Jock says they showed fight for several minutes but after split-arsing around put their noses down and headed for home. He got short burst into one of them but didn't see him go down. Missed, as he always does, he said. Photo shows one he missed on left of snap and also one of Pfalz merchants getting pipped in the backside by Sandy. My turn to get one now.

WEDNESDAY. Kaiser Bill must have visited his fledglings and put some pep into them for they were all up to-day and came well over our lines, not so usual. Tackled two-seater but she got away when her escort dropped into the mess. Had camera with me but did no good as I only caught wing tip of Fokker. Have it pointing back in new position. Jock tried it when he went up this afternoon and came back with a corker. As it came up in the tray chills ran up and down our spines, like a couple of schoolgirls; had snapped a Hun as it was trying to shoot a burst into him, as he came in with two holes in his right wing which entered from rear. Suddenly dawned on us how many times before Huns must have been sitting there trying to pot us and we never knew it. Whoever said ignorance was bliss jolly well knew what they were talking about. Jock says Huns to-day good scrappers, but not unusual, which remark made me laugh. He saw the point and laughed too. In celebration of his narrow escape I stood bottle of fizz.

THURSDAY. Tommie missing. Over on first patrol this morning, which I hate as then sun is in your eyes and E.A. can get close to you unseen, which is just what they did. Before we knew it we were being peppered by tribe of heathen who not only knew how to fly damn well but were not going to let us get chance to pot them. Fight lasted about ten minutes. Got couple of Huns in front of me but missed each time. Finally got rid of them when they climbed away from us. We got none at all but Tommie has disappeared. When those Tripes want to go up *they go up,* and leave us down below as if we had anchors on our tails. No news about Tommie yet. Haven't given up hope yet. Jolly decent chap.

FRIDAY. Washed out after tea and tootled into —— with Jock and Mick. No binge complete without his smiling mug along. Took —— to dinner with us, but she had to leave early for duty, so we finished the evening out ourselves, jolly good time. Old Mick is one of the best, even if he has a smashed-up mug. Really believe if Huns could see his face before they attacked him they would run home with their tails between their legs. Has a face exactly like a bulldog, ferocious to look at, harmless as a kitten and the guts of a lion. One of the best chaps I've met. Got in little while ago, but don't feel tired. Put Jock to bed and Micky sleepy, little tight myself. Here's hoping it pours to-morrow.

SUNDAY. Got two-seater to-day and also damned good snap of it. Wing phoned through that plane was over —— taking photos and ordered us to shoot it down. Just like that! Must have high opinion of our ability! However, spotted blighter working but somehow Wing had (naturally) forgotten to mention scouts lazily wandering above him, archie doing everything but hit them. We climbed off in the direction of —— and slowly got to the east of the two-seater. Hun archie, of course, had to give us away, changed course and sailed after two-seater. As we hoped, scouts were a little late in getting there and we all gave two-seater bursts, doing no damage. That pilot was no novice. In a second sky

89

"Got two-seater to-day"

"A shining example of what not to do"

was mad whirl of lead-spitting planes. In the excitement saw two-seater climb out of the mess and instead of skipping home went about flying over our trenches. Suddenly dawned on me blighter was going to get his pictures or bust. Left rest and stole after him. Obs. saw me and pilot turned frequently to let obs. shoot bursts at me as I followed under his tail. Luckily scouts hadn't seen me as they didn't follow. Put short burst in under his tail, then they decided to get rid of me once for all and continue their work unmolested. Saw the fight going on below me but still no Huns came up to us. Something told me to get the two-seater if I had to dive head-on into him, and I split-arsed around like a wasp with a flea under his tail. Every time I got him in a blind spot pilot would bank and obs. give me a short burst. Tracers sped past me at all angles, and once heard something go with a bang. Took wind out of me for second, but could see nothing hanging loose or broken, and no time to investigate, so kept on. Got beautiful burst in at last from protection of his right wing, and could see tracers burying themselves in his fuselage. As I hung for a second helpless got lovely burst from obs. Two bullets tore through my right boot and toes nearly froze. For a second I lost him, then saw him gliding back to his lines with lost prop. That pilot had guts. Came down on them but obs. gave me another short burst. That made me mad as he must have known I had him helpless. Didn't shoot back but flew up close where obs. gun could not train and pointed towards our lines. Pointed to my gun at same time and shot short burst in case he didn't understand. He made a wide turning hoping, no doubt, that scouts would see his predicament, and slowly glided west over our lines. I kept close in a blind spot and then watched him make beautiful landing in rough ground. What a pilot! Tommies were around in a second, but chumps didn't have enough sense to make them get out with their hands up. As I circled I saw obs. lifting pilot out, then quickly duck into cockpit, second later machine was on fire. Well, I could have killed them but, oh well, what's the use? I had visions of presenting nice two-seater to Wing as live trophy but Huns were too smart for me. Bucked over picture I got, though. Shows Blackie trying to get him from above while I tried to shoot him from the side. Was first home, and sweated blood waiting for rest of flight to come in, but all back. Thought I was down. Said they had filthy fight with escort. Feel in celebrating mood to-night, everyone in good form.

MONDAY. Tried to get in touch with two Huns I brought down yesterday but Wing said pilot had died and obs. turned over to Intelligence. Got his name and sent him a note asking if I could do anything for him. Talk about a worthy foe! Handed him kudos for his and pilot's fighting ability. Have to admit it, they were good. Sent along some gaspers. Jock and I took

advantage of dud day to run into —— and see ——
and get him to make some enlargements for us to work
on. Spent afternoon with —— while Jock worked
with ——.

THURSDAY. Spent entire day retouching and making
snaps real works of art, according to Jock, who is certainly an artist at the job. Takes a pencil and in no time
everything is clear and sharp. The one he took a fort-
night ago was a job, as the planes were so small. Went
into town this evening after tea and —— made copies
for us. Think Jock interested in ——, needs cheering up,
he says! Spends entire time in dark room pointedly sug-
gesting I take old boy out for drinks at estaminet—whole
bottle in fact. Photography interesting recreation! Clear
to-morrow, stars out to-night.

FRIDAY. Hell of a day, but did our damnedest and
flew through storms searching for Huns in every possible
shelter and in the open; caught one batch of them wading
across watery stretch of road and spattered them with
lead. Adding injury to insult! Bullets splashed in water
and helped to correct our aim as we dived on them.
Scared them, they ran in all directions. Poor bloody
beggars. What a life. Saw French troops almost up to
their necks in water but going ahead nevertheless. Waved

and cheered as they saw us dive after some Huns opposite them.

SATURDAY.   Jock down in flames. That would have to happen, and he always dreaded the sight of anyone burning up, no matter if it was a Hun. He sat next to me at mess after Canada was shot down, and now that chair is empty. Farrie says they were attacked by big flight of scouts and before they could get away from them they had lost Jock. Sandy is the only one who saw him go down and says he was killed by a bullet and was dead before he caught fire. How the hell does he know? Probably just being tactful, knowing we were good pals. Bloody heaven.

SUNDAY.   Heavy ground mist, so we kept on with the ground strafing. God, how I hate that work. How I hate everything out here. Forget how many quids my plane is worth including guns and my useless life, but surely something more than a fiver, and they send us up to shoot dirty Huns wallowing in muck and mud; moral effect, of course, and all that bally rot. Great moral effect when you get a bullet in your bottom or bury yourself in six feet of mud, or go down in flames. Canada gone; then The Bard and now Jock. Told we mustn't think about it. Hell! And the fireside warriors at home whine when an occasional bomb tears up their allotment patch and write to *The Times* about "on to Berlin." Bloody lot of Berlin stuff you would hear if those slackers had to come out here and do some fighting. Latrine work is about all they would be able to do successfully.

TUESDAY. Went into —— with Chilly, and Withy. Chilly about due for his squadron, I think, but only smiles when I mention it. Hasn't any friends with influence to give him a boost, so suppose he will die with his boots on and three pips. Met S—— out on D.H.5s. Says they are tricky but strong and likes them after umpteen hours on them. Says they look more ferocious than they really are. Nice for joy riding but twin brother to a stone when engine konks.

WEDNESDAY. Lost another to-day, Scotty, who tried so hard to do what he was told. Perhaps if we had watched over him more carefully he would still be here. Oh, well, all one can do is to forget and carry on. But it's hell, his first time over the lines. Caught rather unusual picture to-day. Here is shining example of what not to do when having a bit of a do with the Huns—*let him get on your tail!* Let us hope that the fledglings from C.F.S. will study this picture long and carefully in the next war and that their instructors will point out the lesson it contains. Wish I could send them a print now! Here is little Scotty, getting pipped for the first time and the last time. Poor little beggar. I had placed the camera to snap backwards and trust to luck if I got anything. I did, and wish to God I hadn't. Makes me boil when I think how they are sending out pilots now, with only a bare five or six hours on a service machine, sheer cold meat for the crowd of Huns we have been up against lately. Don't know what their squadron is but they are a crack lot of pilots and we are having a bloody time with them. Had begun to think I was fairly good pilot, but after Tuesday and to-day when I came home full of Krupp steel my ego is somewhat deflated. Ones in particular which give us the most trouble are a crowd of vari-coloured parrots, but they can fly like eagles. Met up with them to-day and they got that kid Scotty. God knows how many more of us they will collect before we see the last of them. C. Flight got a sausage.

THURSDAY. If this sort of weather is what they get every year at this time here give me the desert. Wonder the inhabitants don't drown themselves in despair. Am going into —— this afternoon, spend the rest of day and evening with ——. To hell with everything.

FRIDAY. Another day of rain and mud, so Blackie and I wandered out for a walk after lunch. Everybody playing bridge or sleeping so had to get out or bust. Watched Tommies handling big heavies. A sight to see. Don't envy life of infantry. Poor bloody fools—as we all are.

WEDNESDAY. Lost another to-day, Tod. Only out here a week or two. Mess sort of fidgety to-night, bad luck sort of depressing. He was damned fine chap, good pilot, too. The Skipper and Woolly are weighing pros and cons by fireplace, sort of lifeless and tense around. Been losing them fast lately, makes one jumpy, especially when we have all been together so long and know each other pretty well. Had all begun to think the Lord was keeping his weather eye on us. What an illusion! Tod was an only child, but you'd never know it, was so jolly decent and sporting in every way. Somehow I always feel it's my fault when they get pipped, it ought to have been me, but that's nerves probably. It's good, of course, to hear what a fine son one *had* but it's the past tense that holds all the damnable meaning, and no amount of eulogising will eradicate that one little word. This war business is all damned rot, and I'm not alone in my opinion. Luckily for the Big Bugs they don't give us much time to think about things, if they did there would be a quick curtain drop and "FINIS", and I

"Tod in the S.E."

believe this applies to both sides. No wonder they doll us up in shining brass and tinkling cymbals at home, make us think it is going to be some fun across the Channel, instead of bloody murder under the cloak of patriotism. Damnation and hell—when I start to think of it I start to drink, to keep my blood at boiling point—ginger myself up to go out and kill and laugh at my conquests. Great for these days of emancipation, when man is supposed to be superior to the beast. I don't think. I almost forgot the picture this morning. Believe when it is dry shall get good print. As we lost one and the Huns lost one it must be Tod in the S.E. at the top of the picture and the Hun in the middle. They must have shot at each other at the same time, because none of us got any. Some of these Rumpler merchants are pretty good and do not need much of an escort of scouts.

THURSDAY. Lovely spinning party this morning with those painted German harlots. Robby sent one spinning down and followed him down. Sure enough foxy Hun came out of spin few hundred feet over the trenches and then Robby got him. But Hun infantry got him properly right after and he limped home on half a cylinder. Lenn and I caught one of them napping and he went down in slow spin but had decency to crash properly to the east of his lines. We decided to split it as Lenn already has half a Hun to his credit and only needed another half to

"His wings suddenly collapsed and floated past me"

make a whole scalp. Too windy to go up this afternoon, so have just developed plate which is throw out. Miss Jock like the devil.

FRIDAY. Just a "wee doch an' doris this bra bricht nicht" as "The Bard" would have said, for this carrion bird of prey celebrateth in humble and crude, withal regal style, for I feel like a king. And who wouldn't, for just after lunch we did get us a corker of a picture. Nearly cost me my useless life, though, for the broken wing of the blighter's plane nearly barged into me. Just swerved in time to miss it by my eyelashes. We had special orders to pick off a Hun two-seater doing some pretty artillery work over near —— and Sol, Lenn, Ferdo and I went up for it. Robby couldn't go as his engine still out of commission. Climbed steadily and watched carefully for Huns overhead but to our surprise saw none. Got lot of attention from Archie, though, they made it uncomfortable for a time. Lenn as usual picked up a lot of it. He is an absolute champion at absorbing hot steel, and never gets it in his tough hide either. Couldn't find the Hun for a while, and circled high over spot where he was reported. Knew he must still be doing his little bit as we could see the shells dropping all around his objective. Too bad those nice, well-mannered German guns can't reach back as far as the Wing! Our batteries were doing something in exchange to divert their interest somewhat, so all in all they must have been having a lovely time downstairs. Ferdo finally found the blighter and we wandered over towards him. Still no sign of life from anyone overhead—seemed too good to be true—so Ferdo, Sol, Lenn and I went down on the Hun with the sun behind us. But old Boche saw us coming, I pulled up without firing and circled over him and could see Lenn trying to get him from above and Ferdo dancing around underneath. (Archie had ceased to function, thank the Lord, and we could enjoy the scrap in peace. That L.V.G. pilot and his obs. were no novices, for every time Ferdo or Lenn would get into a good position he would kick her over and the obs. would squirt juice all over us. How long this state of affairs lasted can't say, but suddenly Hun nosed down and we followed. Ferdo cleared off for home as he had got a burst from Hun in his engine. We came down full engine on and could see obs. reaching over into the pilot's cockpit, apparently trying to pull him off the stick, so he must have been hit, as he was slumped forward. We were diving at terrific speed and I pressed the triggers—just for *bonne chance.* Whether or not I put any lead into him don't know, but just as I was shooting his wings suddenly collapsed and floated past me. He went down like a stone, lower wings flapping off and slowly fluttering down. Ferdo gets credit for that Hun as he managed a long burst into the centre section just before he nosedived. Lenn's plane was riddled and he limped home

102

with his oil pressure almost at zero. As we were too low for archie to bother us we managed to get home in peace. "The end of a perfect day."

SATURDAY. Just another day. Feeling queer last few days, although nothing matter with me. Played chess with Rags to-day, got licked every time. Got jim-jams, can't keep still. Must take hold of myself. Fatal to let oneself go. Going into —— to-night, take —— out to dinner, take my mind off things.

SUNDAY. Steve of B. Flight, said it was his birthday to-day, so we had excuse to celebrate. Anything for an excuse. Toasts to his health and accompanying speeches would have made marble statue blush. Pills had dinner with us. Good fellow. Looked me over once or twice, then asked me how long I have been out. Told him. Said too long. Nervous, need change. Rats, I told him. Don't want change because that means either instructing or cushy job at Air Ministry or something and can't stand sitting down job amongst those Brass Hats.

MONDAY. No news. Letter from obs. I relieved from further worries a few weeks ago. Said he hoped I was still alive and would soon be taken prisoner. Cheery old chap. Sent me his picture taken by one of guards. Said

"Have got the camera pointed off at an angle"

he hadn't heard from his people in Germany yet.

Tuesday. Fairly decent day at last, after mist and rain. Tootled over to northern end of parade ground and didn't see anything for some time. Clouds low. After loafing along about to go home when Huns came through clouds and in second were in hot mix-up. What beautiful birds of prey those Huns were. Caught picture of Phalz diving on one of our flight's tail. No harm done, though, as mess intact to-night. Have got the camera pointed off at an angle just behind me, and while I find I miss a lot, do get a good one occasionally. We had our little mix-up to-day with these Phalz merchants and they are a good average lot of fighters, although to my mind not as effective as the Fokkers. It was more or less of a draw, and after split-arsing around for a few minutes slipped away from them. Sounds rather like white feather, but wasn't, by any means. Wind was carrying us east all the time and petrol was getting low. They also must have been at the end of their fuel as they didn't follow us across the lines. Don't need to keep an eye on Winn as he is more than capable of taking care of himself. Robby must be in the S.E. in the lower part of the picture as he came back with a pretty burst in his fuselage near the fin. Not serious, though.

105

"Kaffir is behind me."

WEDNESDAY. Another hard day. Tired. Incessant ground strafing, rain or no. Patrol time comes too bloody quickly, and even A.M.'s look tired as they tuck us in with a cheery smile and a word of "Good luck, sir." Have good crew mechanics here, work like the devil and always good-natured. Feel sorry for them when buses come in full of holes. They look them over so carefully, bet they almost weep at damage sometimes. Means all night work often, patching and tinkering in hangar. Wander out sometime and have chat with them, send out bottles of beer and gaspers. Rather like to talk with mechanics, have philosophy all their own, pretty sound sometimes. Of course, they are comparatively safe in their jobs, only risk being occasional bomb. But they know our lives depend greatly, if not entirely, on their work. One mistake and a pilot is done for. Damn well they know it, too.

SATURDAY. At last a decent snap. Had almost given up hope of getting damned thing in working order again, every one I got throwout. Cleared up this afternoon enough to fly. Had been over lines about half hour when Fokkers ripped into us. Kaffir and I kept our eyes on Rex but he doesn't need much nursing. Tore around each other for few minutes and I missed good shot but managed to get fair picture at same time. Got camera behind me again where it is out of sight. Kaffir

"Tad split-arsing after one of the Huns"

is behind me, S.E. nearest, while I think Larry is above. I was diving steeply when I pressed triggers and camera snapped pointing vertically into sky. Think everyone, including Huns, feeling tired and a little off. None of us got scratch, am certain Huns didn't.

——DAY. Huns still stubborn and seem to be trying to break through after a little rest. Things seem to be normal, on our section at any rate, although we are hard at it giving Boche little peace. Got bad scare this morning. Just as our flight was about to take off the —— and his brass-hatted chair-warmers drove up in their gilded splendour. Our buses all out on tarmac warming up. Strolled out on to tarmac just as their highnesses alighted from their chariots. The Admiral and Tacks were clicking heels and saluting, and of course Kaffir and I had to stiffen up also. Froze stiff. Caught Pauling's (rigger) eye and he quickly set about examining under part of my wing, as I had unfortunately placed the camera there instead of in fuselage, and slipped with it into hangar, luckily without being seen, though how he managed to hide it, God only knows. Anyhow, gilded youth was probably too thrilled at seeing a front line plane at close quarters for the first time to take notice of anything else! After a lot of yap we took off, without camera. But gods were kind and made up for it this afternoon when we met up with more Fokkers of the biplane type, just above the clouds. Got a short burst into one of them, but don't know whether or not I hit him. We outnumbered the Huns, and after a few minutes split-arsing around they suddenly dived through the clouds. We followed but they got away. Got a good snap of Tad split-arsing after one of the Huns.

——DAY. Kicked our heels until this afternoon when we went over, sky reeking with Huns. Seemed to be waiting for something to shoot at and we got the burst of their spleen. They tried to pick us off like choice hors-d'œuvres, but we must have been tough as we are all here to-night. Something must have gone wrong with the camera as I thought I had got a good snap but plate was blank. Just been looking it over in hangar, gadgets seems to be all right so must be working all right, just bad luck.

——DAY. Mac lost a man this morning in a dog-fight. Felt very blue about it. Burned up. Long time since we had any casualties, begun to think were invulnerable. Mac sitting on edge of his cot now drinking whisky-and-soda one after another, talking it over. He is one of the best, great pilot. No matter how many Huns he brings down still same quiet little Scotsman. Works like the devil, drinks like the devil, and broods like the devil when he loses a man. Mal was his last man out, but by no means fledgling as had been out here some time. Nothing happened to our Flight, thank God.

FRIDAY. Suppose we shall return compliment and do some tough work with —th Squadron. Friend Hun has changed his plans and is hitting them hard up there now. All had little rest, however, and feel fresh for more slaughter.

SATURDAY. Huns still at it. Certainly picked glorious weather to do their pushing in. Half time we are unable to leave ground on account of fog or rain. Keeping fit and resting every chance we get. If we can stand this maybe the end of the war will not be far off. . . . . . . Gave lot more work for us to do as result. They say their Tommies are good but officers n.g. Never met any of them.

MONDAY. Tad killed. Strafing infantry and playing hell with them when I noticed he flew in queer manner. Seemed to have gone mad. Instead of working with rest of us went tearing after Huns in all directions on his own. Then saw him shoot his Very's pistol at them. Knew his ammunition was gone. Suddenly he tore down at them, none of them fell. His guns were silent. Large group was ahead of him and he plunged head on into

"Larry got one of the Fokkers"

them, piling up in a seething mass of mangled arms and legs. He killed them even as he killed himself. Only reason we can think of is that he must have been hit in some place he knew was vital, and knowing he was done for decided to complete job the way he did. He had guts. Feel blue about it. Kaffir is last one of original roster and he can't last much longer. Hell rampant on a field of blood.

WEDNESDAY. Heart-breaking weather to fly in. Spotted Huns in a village square, apparently waiting for billets or something. Maybe beer ration. Some of those poor buggers will need neither beer nor billets again, for we dropped all our bombs on them, and then sprayed them for good measure. Square littered with Huns and they could only pop at us when we were diving on them, as houses sheltered us when we turned. Officers helpless, and after several dives all scattered in doorways. Rex is priceless. Goes right down to within few inches of their heads and literally knocks them over. What more can one ask for out here than to have five bloody good pilots behind you and know they will never let you down.

FRIDAY. Like Christmas for a while to-day, went over in between bad spots, but they turned bad before we got back once. Kaffir showing signs of cracking up.

M.O. will be over to-morrow and the Admiral will get him to look Kaffir over. Too good a man to lose for want of a little rest.

SUNDAY. Quiet, for a while at least. Let's hope it continues. Even Hun pilots seem tired. Had to go far over for them to-day and then they were not disposed to fight until we went at them. Then they had to. Got good illustration for text-book to-day, pure blank! Chased Fokkers out of big formation and they stayed to fight for a few minutes and then buzzed off.

THURSDAY. Early flying, and after two day loaf it *was* early. Saw nothing first half of patrol but spotted Fokkers again, a new squadron, I think, by general markings, etc. Short scrap, and I missed really good shot. Too slow on triggers. Must try some clay-pigeon shooting when get chance. Larry got one of the Fokkers and I think it was one shown in photo I managed to get when I missed mine. Anyhow, whoever it is he is right on the Hun's tail and it is good-bye to him. Short scrap and I was glad of it. Huns suddenly got wind up and buzzed off. Didn't follow as petrol was getting low. One more notch on —— Flight's escutcheon. Mac is going out on his own to-morrow. Thinks he can get more Huns if he is alone—hides in upper layers of clouds.

THURSDAY. Have succeeded in enticing Lady Luck back again so far as getting Huns (in my camera) is concerned, even if I don't get them in person. Saw large formation of them being watched by Camels. Together we outnumbered them, though that is not always sign of success. Camels started it and we went in a minute later. On first burst thought I had a Fokker where it would do him most good, but he must have had cast iron bottom as he blithely faded out of it and carried on. Those Fokkers were hot stuff, and the resulting dog fight long and fierce. Got one off Rex's tail and split-arsed around quietly hoping to get another in range and close up. Either I am a dud shot further than 10 yards or the bullets shoot in circles—don't know. Anyhow, came back with nothing but neat holes in my wing tip to boast of, and they are not archie holes either, and also what —— considers a decent picture. So no grousing.

FRIDAY. Got a good illustration for ———'s text-book to-day. One can show in photograph what would take 1,000 words to explain. But rub is "get the photograph." Three of us up to-day on high patrol and didn't see soul at first. On the south end spotted Camels entertaining Fokker biplanes again, so tore down into it. About over when we got there, and the stein lifters this time had won the cup, but we managed to get in a few bursts each before we all got jumbled up in clouds. I

"A decent picture"

"Little Camel he was diving on"

can't claim for the Fokker although I feel sure that I pipped him, and no one saw me shoot it anyway. Sprayed him liberally, know he must have got some of it. Little Camel he is diving on seemed to be going down out of control, but that may have been my heated imagination. Those Camel "drivers" have neat way of split-arsing on a sixpence that is amusing at times when there are not so many Huns flying about to spoil the game. Damned fool, spilled lot of cigarette ash on negative when wet.

THURSDAY. Only flown few hours in a week, seemed like visiting strange land when we went over lines this morning. Stiff scrap with Hun two-seaters, rest seems to have given them lots of vim. We sent one of them tearing down like fat hen, but didn't see it crash—must have got away. This afternoon again met those Fokker merchants. All the German toy factories must be enlisted into making those planes, see so many of them these days. Kaffir suddenly pulled himself together and eased up on the whisky. Thank the gods. Told me to-night his only brother killed first day of push—rather upset him. Can understand.

FRIDAY. Cleared about tea time to-day and there was hardly room for us all in the sky. Just as well as I got a good photo of a Hun decorating Spad with nice

117

"Hun decorating a Spad"

cross, wooden, not iron. But have got to stage where everything is come and go, and now can collect scraps of executions and burnings without blinking. Always the cup that cheers, and at present can't remember very distinctly what happened when I got picture to-day. Know we saw Fokkers nosing after Spads. Don't blame Spads for showing their tails to that team of Fokkers. Anyhow, believe I got lovely burst into the Hun's fuselage as he tore past me. Spad went careening down in flames minute later, but I didn't see Fokker. Suppose he is home now drinking himself under the table.

TUESDAY. —— flight intact but Mac has lost Rats somewhere. Was with patrol when they came this side of our lines and flying in rear. Going into —— to-night for binge. Not much attraction there any more for me except occasional bust to relieve monotony—change of venue.

WEDNESDAY. If I don't come through this war shall endeavour to get in touch with either Turner or Whistler on the other side and ask them to polish their monocles and cast their optics on the picture I got to-day. Am just cocky with pride at having achieved work of art as well as war souvenir of battle in the air. Exchanged courtesies with some dirty looking Fokkers who stuck

119

"Bristol kicked his tail right in my face as I was in act of
pressing trigger"

their noses into quiet meeting we had arranged with two Bristols. Needless to say, the Bristols got what they were after, in spite of interruption by Fokkers, who incidentally got more than they wanted. Party quite exciting for a while. Pipped Fokker just as he was about to take pot at one of our chaps. Don't know whether I got him or not so can't claim for him. Bloody nearly got wooden cross for myself though, for just missed smashing into one of the Bristols. Sheer carelessness on my part and should be hung for it, although Bristol kicked his tail right in my face as I was in act of pressing triggers at Fokker, and damn it, it shows in the picture and nearly spoilt it. Fokker I was after can be seen just as he was letting go at one of us. Larry got one down out of control. Wish to hell I could work out some scheme where I could take a picture each time I take a pot at a Hun, could then take a dozen each time I am up, instead of only one, and would get bigger collection as surely one out of each time up would show something, whereas it is now blanks for days at a time, then a little run of good luck, perhaps two or three in a week, then more blanks. No casualties to-day. Everything peaceful in mess. Rats got in late this afternoon, dud engine, slept all night in bus. That bit of a pill always comes out right side up and will continue to adorn the mess when rest of us are under the sod, and unable to contradict his tall stories of achievements. Rotten pilot, too, bloody conceited into bargain.

121

"Air all wings and bullets"

THURSDAY. Tired as the devil to-night, worked all day. Over three times, two scraps. Fritz in truculent mood and instead of giving us wide berth took his medicine like a man. Went well over the lines and carefully dropped some eggs on them which hatched on contact. Had to fight almost every inch of the way back the last time over, after tea. Got nothing. My pup has hurt her foot somehow to-day. Beside me now in little box, beginning to know me already and be faithful.

FRIDAY. Kaffir gone. Ripped his wings off about ten miles the other side of ——. We had spotted big Hun formation, sixteen or more in patrol. I watched to see if any of our planes were near us but we had the sky to ourselves and tempted to skip. Climbed higher and kept in the sun and it was some time before Huns seemed to notice us. We dived through them and picked off the ones on the extreme end. But leader was no fool and when we came at him he, with three others was diving after us and they peppered us all. Kaffir must have got hit badly as I saw him continue on down, wings ripping off. Saw two Huns collide and last I saw of them they were going down. Got away from them by getting down on the ground and skipped home. Two of them kept after me, but managed to evade them. Kaffir will be hard to replace, damned good pilot, could be relied on not to let you down. All on edge to-night—wish there was some excuse to buzz into ——. Would go anyhow if it were not that too much drink the night before has bad effect on my flying next day. Otherwise would get blotto and stay blotto, to stop thinking.

SATURDAY.   I miss Kaffir like the devil. Two brushes with Huns, first early this morning when we were diverting attention of persistent Huns from D.H.4s. Had almost reached end of our escort point when Fokkers jumped on us. For a few seconds air all wings and bullets, then suddenly it cleared as flight of Dolphins from nowhere came in. Huns, outnumbered, nosed away, we didn't follow, and Dolphins went upstairs again. Frankly, those big bulldogs saved us from tough scrape. Scrim hit in arm, just scratch. Had camera in fuselage pointing up and off at an angle, got decent photo. After tea had to go far over lines before we saw anything. Affair short but hot while it lasted. Dropped eggs on drome at —— but saw no planes about so presumed Fritz away. Coming back got above clouds and still saw nothing of E.A. Then saw too much. About fifteen, seemed like fifty for a while, were split-arsing around us and I knew that if we wanted to get home we should have to fight with our backs to the wall. They were good lot of pilots and if it hadn't been for Spads which came into scrap few minutes afterwards doubt if we should have got home at all. Grand fight on when

Spads came into it, and we were soon down in the clouds. Tumbling through them saw Fokker in range and pressed triggers. A couple of shots and then silence. Had a jamb. In trying to clear it just missed getting my prop tangled up in a Fokker's tail. Cold sweat. Lewis drum was hit and hopeless. Squirmed out of mess and finally got the Vickers going again and went back in, but it was all over.

SUNDAY. Got replacement this afternoon, American, from ——. Jolly sort of chap. Lent to us *pro tem.* as Americans have no planes of their own worth flying, they say. Trained in England, just from ——. Fortunately have bus for him, and after tea took him over for flip this side of the lines to let him see Front as it really is. Had exciting day, got chased home by big Hun formation. Spotted second formation higher than first, so suddenly decided to turn west. Sometimes discretion is better part of valour! Had to hurry a bit few minutes after, but only got archied. Mac got another to-day. When I get one feel like writing to *The Times.* He just orders an extra whisky. Taffy, seems good poker player.

MONDAY. Got one to-day, also damned good picture. Out over Hunland well above clouds which eased the pain of archie a bit, when those ugly mugs hove in sight. Saw nothing above so tore into them. Larry skipped out towards home. Thought he was hit but turns out he has to have new engine. Limped home pluckily and didn't crack up. Scrim watched Larry's tail damn well as Huns were after him like pack of wolves. When we reached our lines Bristols helped Huns make up their minds they had gone far enough. Plate shows Taffy almost getting pipped. Must have hit my Hun squarely amidships. He went down in a spin and A.A. saw this one so I get it.

WEDNESDAY.   Nothing exciting. Plenty of Huns gave our A.A. lot of work and we had short scrap. No one missing. Somebody brought back lot of new records from London and they are dancing in the next room. Bug's laugh can be heard above all the din, nothing seems to dampen his spirits. Mac tells me is positive wild-cat in scrap. Two weeks or so ago both his guns jammed and when he landed he was crying with sheer unalloyed rage. Has three Huns to his credit in short time he has been here. Amusing kid.

THURSDAY.   Camera hit, but Liam says he can fix it up for me. Had conceit knocked out of me this morning. In an argument over near —— two Huns gave me their undivided attention to the extent that I am *hors-de-combat* until to-morrow at least. Had new streamers on which perhaps caught their eye and they made me dance

126

like a grasshopper in a frying pan. Got couple of bullets in my engine and were it not for Ling and Scrim who watched my tail while I got away would be drinking Münchner to-night if lucky enough to be down alive. Have been waiting to get piece of archie or bullet in camera for some time. Serves me right for thinking about it so much. I got it.

FRIDAY. Getting bored with everything, also unusually lazy. Stayed in camp until after lunch and then washed out for the day and went into —— where we all had a real hot tub of water. Convent where we go is an old affair and the nuns who have charge of the baths are nearly as old as the convent! After every visit I usually wander into the chapel and look around at the quaint old place, so peaceful. Strange how a church will affect one at times. Here is a world plunged in the last stages of hate and destruction and within range of the larger guns is a chapel where the nuns go about as if they had never heard of war. They have faith, at least, and infinite peace of soul, or anyhow they seem to have. Makes me feel cheap when I think of the all too many times when I have felt shaky in a tight place. One can learn a lot from those nuns, a "peace which passeth all understanding." At night they are bombed, only last week one landed in a little orchard at the back of the convent, and still they kneel and pray, and work, tend the sick, cheer the gloomy, their faces like rays of sunshine in a black hell. One nun in particular, a young girl whom I first saw when I was last there, only young one I've seen, reminds me of stories of Joan of Arc. Saw her again to-day. Came into the chapel while I was there and sat in a pew near me. I watched her, wondering why such a beautiful young girl should want to give up the world and be a nun. She looked up and saw me looking at her, and smiled. There was something in the utter beauty and serenity of that smile which got under my skin. Sort of made me feel that if I were shot to-morrow I don't believe it would hurt so much as it would have done to-day. Silly.

SATURDAY. One of those days when you have to hang around the mess waiting for the weather to make up its mind whether to be too rotten to fly or clear up enough to go up. Did both alternately all day, so that just when you are buried in the climax of a good detective story and are tempted to look at the last page to see who did it, you have to drop it and go over. And when you get over the lines you run into a bloody squall and can't find the lines, or see about fifteen fat Huns which, on chasing, turn out to be one lone wet hen of an R.E.8. with Christian Scientist crew blandly waving cheerio to you. And to cap it all, when you come home after nearly crashing up when landing in too soft a spot, you slip on the loose boards bridging the lake outside the ante-room door, spilling your box of gaspers you bought just before going up, in the slimy pool, to find the new chap in somebody else's flight reading your detective story.

SUNDAY. Ran into E—— to-day in the estaminet near the —— dump. Had few drinks together and happened to ask why the devil he didn't transfer to a Bristol Squadron. Laughed at me and said if he had his regular observer with him he would take on any Hun. Of course, he is right, I suppose, in a way, as it is not always speed and climb and manœuvrability that counts but *knowing how* to handle your bus.

MONDAY. Ginger got a Blighty to-day. Was on the tarmac playing with the pup when A. Flight came in. All landed nicely but one of the buses did not turn into the hangar but stayed out on the field, engine slowly turning over. Sensed something wrong and with some A.M's. ran out to it. Ginger was slumped forward and as we lifted him out he opened his eyes and then fainted again . . . . . . poor devil, a Blighty alright. Got him down to —— and they said he would probably live. But he will be out of this mess for a long time. Poor old Tuddy, he'll be sorry about this as Ginger was one of his best men. He's due back in few days. *C'est la guerre.*

"We got away as best we could"

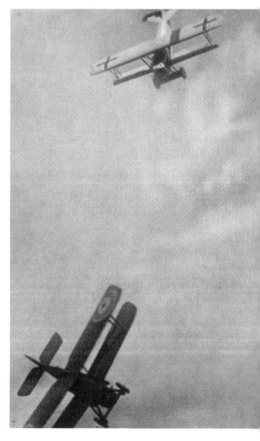

"Good photo of Rex and Fokker"

TUESDAY. Camera going again at last. Damned glad as I've lost good many ripping opportunities for good pictures. What a lot of damage and trouble one little bullet can cause, even in my camera! Lovely day, plenty of Huns up, but my luck not to have a scrap until late this afternoon. After tea went over and got chased out of the sky for our trouble. Ran into big Hun formation and after flirting with them for a while tackled them. In a second we were being tickled in our ribs and toes, and cold chills were running up and down our spines. Had made the mistake of mixing up with lot of old hands, and were outnumbered three to one into the bargain. Had fondly hoped that end ones might be novices, *but they were not.* We got away as best we could, our tails between our legs, but still able to wag at that, which is saying something for ourselves.

WEDNESDAY. On early patrol this morning . . . . . . When we reached the Front and turned for the northern end of the patrol I got the Flight between myself and the rising sun and pressed the camera trigger. Wanted picture of patrol and got one, by God. Like it better than any other picture I have. Scrim is in lead, Larry to his left rear, and at right edge of picture Ling. On Scrim's rear right is Rex and then Taffy. Got a picture that is worth quids to me. Means more than any of the others. Shows daily patrol, which will remain a memory long

"Had camera in fuselage pointing off and up at an angle"

"Wanted picture of patrol and got one"

after the various scraps have faded into a blur. If I had waited two minutes longer to snap that photo would have caught archie bursts which came unpleasantly close.

THURSDAY. Fokker bi-planes are more plentiful every day. Must have taken a tip from Henry Ford. They are no joke though. Am slowly coming to the conclusion that fighting now is not what it was some time ago by any means. Swapped bumps with a tough lot of them to-day and while we didn't get any of them or they us, did get pretty good snap. Rex is damned good pilot, reliable, flies like a veteran. Can see him at the top of the picture. Big Hun at right is one I tried to get from underneath but he was too wily.

FRIDAY. Decided to bring down six or seven Huns to-day on my own! Saw dazzling Rumanian or Armenian decoration on one of gilded staff which would solve problem of dog collar for my pup. After patrol had "RIP" filled up and reloaded and was just about to take off Rex blew along and asked what it was all about. Told him my ambitions, he said he'd always hankered after pretty ribbon for a garter, so came along too. Waited in shelter of clouds for something awkward and easy to come along, and it did. But they were neither awkward nor easy. Far from it. Jockeyed into favour-

"God, what a sight"

able position and then ripped into them. Soon realised we were in a fight that was not going to be easy to get out of. For few minutes were kept busy trying to preserve our hides. Decided that Rumanian decorations were not good enough for my pup, the piece of string suits him better. Threw "RIP" around cruelly in effort to get out of the mess, and after what seemed hours of torture managed to shake them off. Got in several bursts during melée but they must have had cast iron shirts as they absorbed the bullets and came back for more. Realised that if I wanted any pretty ribbons would have to join the Staff instead of getting shot full of holes by Huns. Licking was not without its brighter side as I got damned good photo of Rex and a Fokker. Rex had four neat holes in his fuselage, so he must have been given them by the Hun at the top of the picture.

SATURDAY. Not much rest these days. Fighting in the air has got to be a cold matter of business routine. No longer sportive! Sorry in a way. But the war has to be won, I suppose. We got a Hun to-day after a long scrap, a two-seater. Scrim got it. Didn't get a picture, a blank. Tuddy back from leave. Says London full of Americans who have joined Air Force in Canada. If they are anything like the Americans in the Lafayette Escadrille it won't be long now. Met some of them in Paris, jolly good crowd, plenty of pep.

135

SUNDAY. God, what a sight. Can still hear crash of impact. Scrap started over Bristol which was doing shoot over near ——. We were above Bristol when Fokkers hove in sight, and without waiting to see what was what dived on Bristol. All got there together, and for second air was tight jumble of wings and tails. Impossible to try to hit anything, to get out for air and flying room was first thing. When I finally did get on a Hun's tail and pressed the triggers I saw the Bristol out of the corner of my eye swerve past me and then an awful rending crash. Looked back and saw the two planes locked in a death grip, and as I kicked over to avoid another Hun's fire saw both of them go down, breaking apart. Scrim didn't see it actually happen but saw it going down afterwards. He said he had shot a Hun, got a good burst into his cockpit, but Hun didn't go down, seemed to nose up and then dive as if under control. More than likely Hun Scrim hit was either killed outright or knocked unconscious and plane was flying wild when it crashed into the Bristol. No one will ever know. The Admiral wild about the picture, danced around in his excitement. Bucked about it myself. Gives you something to think about when it's all over!

TUESDAY. Dashed into —— this afternoon and —— made some enlargements for me. Heavy mist on way home and driver got lost for a while, until an Australian Tommie commandeered our tender in exchange for putting us on the way again. Those chaps certainly are amusing, absolute disregard for A.R. or orders or things like that, undisciplined according to our ideas, but good stuff all the same. Hear they pay no attention to any officers but their own. Rather funny. Like to watch a meeting between them and some of our gilded staff. Be worth watching.

THURSDAY. Larry got a Blighty to-day, hit by machine-guns from ground. Just plain hard work to-day and no glory. Low ceiling and we strafed a lot of ground targets with bombs. Got shock when saw Larry wobbling in a funny way, obviously hit. He was, and he came out of it but didn't strafe any more. Came back with us and kept in formation until we landed, stout fellow. Good scout, he carried on. Am proud of his spirit. Anyhow, he'll get good rest in hospital now, at home. After M.O. fixed him up I helped Mac pack his kit and we all chatted with him until he was taken off. Bloody awful to see one of your pals taken away like that. Shouldn't look at it like that, I suppose, he's damned lucky to be alive, but I hate to see them go. The gods certainly are kind to me in the men they have given me to fight with. Larry was quite cheerful, and made me promise to do my damnedest. . . . . . . How in hell can

Huns win with men like that against them?

Friday. Rumour hath it that we are to take up our beds and walk. Van, of B. Flight, is all upset as he has met some "beautiful French girl" in the village. Swears he is going to get a Hun in the morning to pay them out for causing such a heart break. Suppose we shall have some hot work. . . . . . . Tuddy is damned sure we shall. May the angels which fly under our wings not desert us when that time comes.

——day. Bill from Tuddy's flight is gone. Only casualty to-day but bad one for he was a good man. The French are certainly giving the Boche hell for his strafe on our front. Those 75's of theirs spit fire like machine-guns, and are lined up hub to hub almost. Friend Fritz was up strong to-day and we had stiff scrap with one lot of them. A. Flight was flying below us and we were up in the cold watching for the high ones. Some Camels were even higher than we were. Saw flashing of many wings miles off to the north-east and soon spotted what looked like the entire German Air Force heading south. They had seen us and came around in a big sweeping movement. Funny how one's thoughts work at such times. Queer things one thinks of. Must be nerves.

Thought of Spanish Armada and of how it must have looked to our little Fleet. The Camels came closer to us and Tuddy was coming higher every minute. Then one of the biggest dog-fights I have ever been in was on. Why none of us collided is a mystery. Managed to get to the outside, and with one of the Camels tried to pip one of the Huns. We circled and I soon found that he could do tighter ones than I could ever hope to. So I slipped under him and hung on my prop and tried to get him, but he had seen that done before, and when I pressed the triggers he was not there to stop the bullet. That chap was good, and once when he passed me he smiled, and a second later was giving me a short burst. I got out of it and found two Huns on top of me. Some of my flight dropped on them from still higher up and I got out of it. Saw one of our S.Es. go down in flames. A minute later a Hun spun out of the mess and I saw smoke trailing it. I got a burst in another Hun by sheer accident and saw him dive towards his lines. How long fight lasted don't know, but when we came low Huns had slipped away and we finished the patrol. . . . . . . Flight got together and saw Scrim was missing. All the way home was thinking of him going down wrapped in flames. As we landed he stepped out of the orderly room. Almost threw my arms round him, but felt sick when we heard A. Flight had lost Bill. Tuddy very blue about it. Know only too bloody well how he feels. But it wasn't his fault, ... Scrim left fight at start as he got pipped in his engine and limped

"Gas and H.E. and bombs all mixed up in a seething pot of destruction"

home on one cylinder, he says. Snap shows I didn't miss Hun by much, but a miss is a miss even in the air.

——DAY. Never knew time when big pushes were in really ideal weather, and yet we are expected to do our damnedest to stop them from bringing up troops and munitions and keep Hun pilots from doing the same to ours. A compliment to us, no doubt. Lost another chap, from B. Flight. Didn't know him much as he wasn't out very long. It is hell, ground strafing and impossible at times to see the lines on account of shell smoke. Racket is terrific. Back and forth all day long, just time to get a snatch of rest, bite of food, fill up and then over again with more bombs and bullets. Did not take camera to-day. Thank the Lord can load holder and develop in my little contraption. Damn handy this time.

TUESDAY. If Fritz can stand the strafing he is getting these days he deserves all the praise we can give him, war or no war. His artillery was terrific last but the blasting he is being handed now must be driving him potty. Gas and H.E. and bombs all mixed up in a seething pot of destruction, and when one can see through the clouds of smoke the Germans on the ground look like insects moving around on a hot iron. But they are carrying on, and to-day Spads helped us in a scrap with

141

"Managed to get a fair picture"

"With one of the Camels, tried to pip one of the Huns"

Fokkers. Caught a fair picture in the fracas but was not very happy during the fight as I hate to be in the line of trajectory of shells. One Fokker went tumbling down into the mess below, and one of the Spads. Fortunately we all got back nearly whole, just few patches necessary.

THURSDAY. Low ceiling but all went up and played hell with P.B.I. Mess intact to-night, fog over everything like blanket. Pup is sick—now for some real worry.

FRIDAY. Nothing worth writing about. Nearly broke wing tip on drome when turning. Wind got under it. Damn careless, damn tired, damn fed up.

SUNDAY. Had thought we would have a little "let up," but nothing doing. Such fond hopes not to be fulfilled yet awhile. Went over and through mist spotted Fokkers and Spads. Don't know how long they had been at it but when we came in Huns suddenly dived and disappeared in ground mist. Managed to get a fair picture but —— can't think what it would illustrate. His first suggestion would hardly do for dignified text-book. Has actually started work on it—showed it to me to-night—one little paragraph and some sketches of women's heads in the margin. Certainly is prolific writer.

143

THURSDAY. Ground strafed and on way home ran into shower. All landed safely, glad to get down. Another American came in to-day. Comes from ——. ...... Had long chin-wag with him this evening. Interesting chap. Travelled quite a lot. Says he has to get at least two Huns to fulfil promise to his governor. Is strict teetotaller. Had wanted to join up two years ago but family insisted he wait to see what Wilson did. Told me there are so many Germans in America (and Irish too —also rabidly anti-British)—who have great voting power, which is reason America took so long to make up its mind—otherwise would have been over here soon after *Lusitania* went down. Said many American families divided amongst themselves when war broke out, some for us, some for Germans. Cited interesting case of family he knows in America, man married twice, a German, first wife died in Germany and children left there when he came to this country. Married again over there. Result, has three children by first wife fighting with the Germans, and two sons by second wife fighting with American Army. Queer situation. Wonder how Papa feels. Should imagine American Intelligence would have its hands full. Interesting subject for debate—Is blood stronger than patriotism? Have never given subject thought myself. American E.F. will probably prove the point.

MONDAY.   Tackled balloon to-day and got worst of it. Those crews must be able to smell us when we take off to get them. All got back, something to be thankful for. Don't want any casualties to start out with. Breck quite *au fait* with Front now, and Scrim says he is fast developing into good pilot. Ling taken prisoner whilst I was away. Huns dropped note over our lines to say he was alright, not hurt. New chap, Canadian, taken his place. Talked with him just before dinner. Admitted he was a year under age, but that as he is so tall recruiting sergeant must have winked the other eye. From what I saw of his work to-day, and from what Scrim says should say is natural born pilot, so still have good flight. . . . . . . What more can fellow want. Thank God haven't been saddled with any of those heavy-handed merchants. Pup jumped all over me when I got back—bright little beggar, quite devoted, which suits me very well.

THURSDAY.   Bloody day for our squadron with a vengeance. Quite a few E.A. around and B. and C. Flights went up together. Tacks had to phone for more pilots later. Two we know are dead and Breck is missing. Rex, who was one of my best, and Barry of B. Flight are both gone. No one saw Breck go down so we are not sure where he is. No reports from our archie or infantry so far and it is now 2.30. If he came down anywhere near our lines he should have been reported by

"Had glorious (?) fight all by ourselves"

this time. Still, one hopes on in this bloody war, and goes on hoping. Met our Fokker friends again to-day and had glorious (?) fight all by ourselves. Got four of them, one of which is credited to me, so I feel wonderful, oh wonderful. Yes, by God, wonderful, that's the word. Three men gone, and all we can do is to sit here impotent against those God-blasted powers that mow down men like those three. Sit here and choke down whisky until it chokes us because it's all we can do. Sit here and gloom because we can't do anything about it, and swill down whisky because we don't want to think ahead—not pleasant prospect. Sit here and sop it up so that we'll see six vacant chairs instead of one or two, and then start laughing because you can see the funny side of it all, because if you don't laugh you'll go potty or something, and after all, what's the use of anything these days except just carrying on. They're out of it and we damn soon will be, so why worry. As we got four and probably lost three we are one up on the Hun anyway. Our flights were stepping along God's highway in the bright sunshine above the feathery clouds (Shakespeare probably) in the hope of not seeing any Huns to spoil a pleasant patrol, and then we did just that very little thing. Had no choice in the matter, so watched them. They were below us so we slipped into the sun and went down on them. Just as I was about to shoot a nice one he slipped away from me and I flopped around like a clumsy hen, trying to find an inexperi-

147

"He got his Hun"

enced Hun! But apparently they were all *au fait* to-day with the gentle art of fighting, so I made up my mind I had to fly or be flopped. Got a Hun in my ring sight several times, but never for long enough to shoot. Managed after a while to attract the attention of a fellow with the letter P on his wing. Evidently the feeling was mutual for we climbed around each other in the most approved style, showing off for all we were worth. I tried a little trick H—— had pounded into my thick nut at ——, the beer boy made the expected move and I pipped him. The photo shows the Hun just before he dropped down in a spin and then burst into flames. Stupidly, I was watching him go down when I heard that all-too-familiar sound and just turned over in time to miss following in Fritzie's footsteps. No chance to rest on one's oars in this fracas. I was kept busy trying to avoid this new Hun when somebody pipped him for me —think it was Mac—and I found myself in a cloud. That cooled my ardour for any more fighting and climbing up I saw the Fokkers had disappeared and *there were only three of us lost!* Bloody gloomy around here to-night. Even after all this time we don't seem able to laugh with a vacant chair in the mess. Maybe after ten more years of this we shall be able to achieve that enviable state of callousness.

FRIDAY. Breck came back this morning unhurt. Lost

his direction in the fight yesterday and came down near ——. Got help, and landed a second time. It was dusk, and was not sure which side of the lines he was on. Afraid to enquire and slept in bus all night. Before dawn scouted around and heard planes starting up few hundred yards away. Hid until they took off, then found it was our flight! Poor devil had landed in a field on the other side of the village. Seems to me he should have known he was this side of the lines if he had listened to the gun fire, but it was getting foggy and suppose that dampened sound. We can only claim for two Huns yesterday. No one saw Rats's "Hun" go down, and personally don't believe he even shot at one. The speckled Fokker we all saw go spinning out of the scrap was chased by Breck well into his lines. In coming back Breck got lost. When I think of Rex and Barry gone west while that little white-livered bounder Rats never gets a scratch, I see red. Damn well never looks for one if truth were known. Keeps well out of it every time. Seen him, and Mac says same, but what can one do? Can't prove he's windy. But Mac is going to see to it that he gets some of the experiences he brags about so much elsewhere.

SUNDAY. Well over the lines to-day before we saw anything, and were on our way back when we saw fight over towards ——. Dashed over, to find Camels fighting like tigers with lot of Fokkers. Went into melée and got one burst into diving Hun just as they slipped down and away. Had camera with me, and it looks as if friend Boche was not on receiving end of my burst. Most likely the Camel was, but didn't see it when I shot at the Hun. Asked Tacks to phone through to —th Squadron, and they say they have lost no one to-day. Not pleasant thought to think you might have hit one of your own men. Not by a long shot. Plate slightly light struck.

WEDNESDAY: Fairly quiet day. Went over in odd spot of good weather but hung around ante-room most of time. Worked on retouching this afternoon, washed out after tea and spent evening in —— getting copies made and generally mooching around the place. Don't feel very sociable these days. Miss —— like the devil, good little panacea for the blues.

SATURDAY. My guardian angel hasn't deserted me yet. And one look at the picture I got to-day shows why. Got a hurry call to shoo a two-seater away from over —— but when we got there she had, of course, buzzed off. Waited around for a while then decided to come home. But noticed archies bursting all around some E.A. and watched their wings flashing in the sunlight. Altered course and climbed east. Fritz A.A. began to give

"Most likely the Camel was, but didn't see it when I shot at the Hun"

us some attention. Counted eight Huns but decided to let them alone, when spotted bloody two-seater we were after sneaking back over the lines. Signalled Scrim and Bossie and we went after the blighter like three devils kicked out of Heaven. Glanced back and Fokkers were right on our tails. Decided there was just a cat in hell's chance of our getting the beggar before the scouts could catch us. Like a stupid fool I over-shot the two-seater, but Bossie managed a burst into it and she nosed home. Then in for nice set-to with Fokkers. Missed one good chance, but luckily they were only an average lot of fighters. Scrim pipped one and I saw it go down in flames. One clumsy blockhead nearly barged into me once and it took the wind out of my sails for a moment. Three of them kept me on the jump and couldn't shake them off, even though I turned "RIP" inside out. Caught glimpse of Scrim and Bossie fighting like gladiators. Suddenly got on the tail of one of the Huns and got in a short burst but couldn't watch him. Didn't see him any more so must have hit him. Were few hundred feet over Hun trenches when Fokkers left us. When we landed Tacks rushed out from orderly room to know why the hell we hadn't got it. The damn thing was over —— again! Why didn't we get it? Well, why? But Mac and Van were warmed up and took off after it, and Mac, lucky beggar, got it.

"Plate slightly light-struck"

SUNDAY. One patrol this morning, no news of interest. Had letter from Kaffir's mother, asking for "minutest details of how he was shot down." Awful job, can't tell her bare facts, probably upset her no end. Told her all she should know for her peace of mind in first letter, that he was one of the best and finest men, damned true, but can't think why mothers and wives so often want to know exact details.

"Their laugh will no longer be heard in the mess,
The clink of their glasses in silent toasts,
The scream of their wires 'neath deadly stress,
The roar of their motors, their boyish boasts.
THEY'RE GONE."

EXPLANATORY NOTES

A.

A.A.	Anti-aircraft batteries.
A.A. Bursts.	The explosion of anti-aircraft shells. German bursts black, British bursts white.
A.A. Puffs.	Bursts of anti-aircraft shells.
Albatros.	A fast German single-seater pursuit plane or scout.
A.M.	Air mechanic. Fitters, riggers, armourers, *etc.*; in short, the non-commissioned personnel of a squadron.
Ante-room.	Lounge attached to an officers' mess.
A.R.	Army Regulations.

B.

Bagging.	Hunting expression meaning to capture, get, or kill.
Bally.	Polite slang for "damned" (adjective).
Barged.	Collided with or struck. Also met.
B.E. (quirks)	British Experimental. An early type of British two-seater, used for artillery reconnaisance and photographic work. Very slow. Nicknamed "quirks."
Biffo.	Slang, meaning anything sudden, a jolt.
Binge.	Slang term for a wild party or a drinking party.
Blighty.	Slang word for home, or England. Also term applied to wound severe enough to necessitate sojourn in hospital in England.
Blind Spot.	The area which is not visible from the pilot's seat

	or the observer's cockpit. Also term applied to spot from which the observer's gun cannot be fired, such as directly through wires or struts. Gun cannot be fired through such spots even though an enemy plane is visible for fear of shooting away parts of them on observer's plane.
Blotto.	Slang term for drunk. "One over the eight" is also slang term applied to one who had misjudged his capacity.
Boche.	Another term for the German.
Bottom Flight.	Squadrons often flew in layers, one flight at the ceiling, another about two miles high, the bottom flight near the ground. Done for protection of the bottom flight which would harass the ground targets.
Bowden Control.	Device consisting of flexible steel wire encased in flexible metal covering to convey mechanical impulses. Used in operating the triggers of the machine-guns.
Brass Hats.	Staff officers wore gold braid and gold on hat, thus becoming known as "brass hats."
Bristols or Bristol Fighters.	A fast British two-seater, considered by many pilots the greatest fighting aeroplane of the war. Used for all purposes, even as scouts.
Brush.	Short skirmish or brief fight.
Bumpy.	Rough, puffy air.
Burst.	Term applied to the firing of a machine-gun, the usual burst being of ten bullets, but often gun was fired in a burst of four or five bullets, sometimes a long burst. Risk of a jamb, however, was greater when firing long bursts.
Bus.	Aeroplane.
Bust.	Slang term for "exploded" or "burst." (Not an A.A. burst.)
Buzzed.	Went.

Buzzed off.	Went away. Slang.
Blighter.	Slang term applied to one who is a pest, a nuisance, a source of irritation.

C.

Camels.	A very efficient British scout plane designed by Sopwith, improvement on Sopwith "Pup." All Sopwith types were named after some zoological specimen, *i.e.*, Pup, Camel, Dolphin, Snipe, *etc.*
Ceiling.	The limit of a plane's ability to climb.
C.F.S.	Central Flying School.
Chalk-up.	To record.
Chums.	Friends.
Cook's Tour.	When a pilot first arrived at a Squadron in France he was afforded several opportunities to fly near the front lines in company with an experienced pilot to give him a chance to learn the lay of the land. These trips were nicknamed "Cook's tours."
Cooties.	Body lice, prevalent in the trenches during the war.
Crash.	The wrecking of an aeroplane, usual damage being broken propellor or undercarriage, complete demolition being described as a "write-off."
Cushy.	A soft place or an easy job.

D.

T.B. D.B. }	Abbreviations used by the diarist. It is presumed they were used to differentiate between a pressure on triggers when merely warming gun, for which he had special trigger made, and pressure on triggers when he meant to kill enemy. Although no mention is made of what the letters stand for, it is believed that t.b. means test burst, and d.b. means death burst.

159

Dervishes.	Wild, or excited. Derived from the wild dancing Dervishes. Abandoned or mad.
D.F.W.	A German two-seater plane.
D.H.4 or D.H.	A big British two-seater plane designed by De Haviland, used for general two-seater work, and especially for daylight bombing. Had a high ceiling, and very fast.
D.H.5	A de Haviland single-seater scout plane, very fast and very tricky, the top wing being placed further back than the lower one. Could dive very fast, but its eccentricities caused it to be known as "The Flying Coffin."
Dolphins.	A British scout plane, designed by Sopwith.
Duck.	To drop down quickly.
Dud.	An unexploded shell. Also a term applied to anything not good or perfect. A "dud" landing, for instance, means a poor landing, or a "dud" pilot means not a good pilot. A "dud" day would be when flying was impossible on account of the elements.
Duds.	Slang for clothes. Not to be confused with dud.
Drums.	The cylindrical magazine to hold bullets on the Lewis gun.

E.

E.A.	Enemy aircraft.
Eggs.	Bombs.
Empennage.	That part of a plane at rear of fuselage containing fin, rudder, stabilizer and elevators.

F.

Fitter.	The mechanic who had charge of the engine One fitter was assigned to each pilot.

Flight.	A sub-division of a Squadron. Each Flight was usually commanded by a Captain: the Squadron Commander being a Major.
Flopped.	To be shot down or crashed.
Flop.	To fly around in a clumsy fashion.
Foxy.	Cunning, wily, like a fox.
Fuselage.	Main body of a plane containing the motor, pilot's seat, *etc.*

G.

Gone west.	Killed. (Slang.)
Groggy.	Semi-conscious or ill.
Ground-strafing.	The shooting up of infantry, artillery or any other targets on the ground by aeroplanes. Work which was not relished by the pilots.
Guts.	Slang term for fearlessness, or nerve.

H.

Halberstadt.	A German scout plane. There was also a Halberstadt two-seater.
Heavies.	Heavy artillery batteries.
Hedge-hopped.	To fly a few feet from the ground.
H.E.	High Explosive. Ammunition of tremendous destructive power.
H.E.	Home Establishment. Duties with the Royal Flying Corps in England. Many front line pilots were sent back to England after a lengthy period with a fighting squadron in France for light duties to afford them a period of rest. Wounded pilots after convalescence were put on similar light duties until recovered enough to return to France. This must not be confused with the customary leave.
Hun.	A term for the German.

161

Jamb.	Breakdown in the operation of a machine-gun, usually caused by defective ammunition.

Lewis Gun.	A very light and rapid machine-gun used by the infantry and adapted, like the Vickers gun, for aeroplane purposes. It could not be synchronized to fire through the propellor but was used in tractor planes on the top wing and by the observer in the rear cockpit. All the Allied planes mentioned herein were of the tractor type.

Merchant.	A slang term for pilot.
Mess.	The main room of the officers' quarters, especially applied to the dining-room, also to the evening meal. But often used to denote the ante-room or lounge.
M.O.	Medical Officer.
Mooching.	Slang for ambling, wandering about aimlessly.
Mugs.	Slang for faces.

Napping.	Sleeping or dozing. Caught unawares.
N.G.	No good.
Nieuport.	A single-seater pursuit plane designed by the French but also used by the British.

Observer. Obs. }	The second man in a two-seater plane who handled the mobile rear gun and kept a watchful look-

162

out for E.A. while the pilot flew the plane and operated the wireless or took photographs of enemy positions.

O.K.	Term applied to direct hit on a target.
O.P.	Offensive Patrol. Means an offensive patrol carried out over enemy territory.

P.

P.B.I.	Poor bloody infantry. Applies mainly to the men in the trenches.
Pipped.	Shot or hit by a bullet.
Pot.	To shoot at.
Potted.	Shot at.
Predic.	Predicament.
Prop.	The propellor of an aeroplane.
Puggy.	This term can be applied equally to one who is fat or one who is pugnacious, though usually used in the former meaning. Slang.
Pup.	A single-seater plane designed by Sopwith, used by British. Very easily manœuvred.

Q.

Quirk.	Nickname applied to a British Experimental aeroplane.

R.

R.E.8.	Reconnaisance Experimental No. 8. A British two-seater, a little faster than a B.E. and used for same purpose. Superseded gradually by Bristol Fighters towards the end of the war.
Rigger.	The mechanic assigned to each pilot to care for the aeroplane, with the exception of the engine and machine-guns. Fitters care for the engines and armourers for the guns and bombs.

RIP.	Name the diarist gave his aeroplane. He always humorously maintained that as in all probability his plane would be his headstone the name was particularly applicable—*"Requiescat in Pace."*

S.

Scouts.	Single-seater planes.
S.E.5.	Scout Experimental No. 5. A fast British single-seater.
Side-slipping.	Manœuvre of a plane in which it descends with wings almost vertical and fuselage nearly horizontal.
Skidding.	Side-slipping or slipping.
Skipped.	Ran away.
Spotted.	Slang for saw, sighted.
Split-arsing.	Vulgar term used only by pilots for flying at all angles, looping, rolling and upside down. Technical term is aerobatics, which were taught at Ayr, in Scotland.
Spad.	S.P.A.D. forms the name of a French aeronautical concern which designed this single-seater scout plane. There were also Spad two-seaters. This scout plane was used by both the French and the British.
Stall.	Manœuvre of a plane when it loses flying speed, caused as a rule by pulling nose up too high.
Stick.	The lever affixed vertically just in front of pilot's seat by which he controlled the elevators and ailerons. Became known as "joy-stick."
Sun—(out of or into).	The manœuvre by which planes got the sun directly behind them when diving on an enemy plane. The glare of the sun made it almost impossible to be seen until they were right on the enemy planes.

164

Streamers.	Long pieces of coloured cloth which flight leaders attached to wing struts which enabled rest of flight to identify them easily and quickly.

T.

Tarmac.	The ground immediately in front of the hangars.
Taxi-ing.	Term applied to plane when moving on the ground.
T.B.	See under D.B. of these notes.
Tender.	A motor conveyance used for transporting officers and men and light freight to and from comparatively short distances. Used primarily for short runs, but were also capable of and used for long distances.
Tight.	Slang term for intoxicated.
Tootling.	Ambling along, flying slowly and "at ease."
Tracers.	Luminous bullets used to enable pilots to see where their shots were going. Usually every third or fourth bullet fired from a gun was a tracer.
Tractor plane.	A plane with propellor and guns in front of wings. All the British types of plane mentioned herein were of the tractor type.
Tripes.	A triplane designed by Sopwith, used by British. A single-seater. Fokker also designed a somewhat similar one and the Fokker Tripes were very popular with many German pilots. They climb very fast but are slow on dive. Very manœuvrable.
Twigged.	Understood, comprehended.

V.

Vickers.	The machine-gun of that name used on aeroplane when firing through the propellor; a gear known as the C.C. gear, invented by Constantinescue, operated it, and enabled the pilot

	to shoot between the revolving blades of the propellor. First used in spring of 1917.
Verey's Pistol.	A heavy, smooth bore pistol firing signal cartridges.

W.

Warm-up.	Stationary engines had to be run for some minutes before being taken up, to get them to the correct temperature. Also a machine-gun had to be fired frequently at high altitudes to keep the oil from getting stiff and thus preventing the operation of the gun. The British invented non-freezing oil late in the war to overcome jamming of machine-guns when cold.
Wind-up.	Frightened, alarmed.
Wing.	The Royal Flying Corps was divided into groups of several Wings which latter were composed of several squadrons. The Staff (or Brass Hats) of the Wing controlled operations of the various squadrons under its jurisdiction, planning escorts of scouts for bombing expeditions and the protection of photographic and artillery two-seaters. To a very great extent all orders under which a squadron acted emanated from the Wing under whose control it was placed.
Wonky.	Same as "groggy." (Slang.)
W.O.	Wash-out. Order to discontinue duty or work in hand. Also term applied to describe condition of anything as being unfit for further use.
Won, or win.	Slang term meaning to obtain something without permission, to take without asking.
Write-off.	Term applied to an aeroplane which is so badly damaged that it can never be used again. Term gradually came to be used generally in connection with anything which had to be written off the records as being no longer of use.